Triads

of the

Harmonic Major Scale

on Guitar

Copyright © 2022 Alexander Badiarov

- https://www.youtube.com/c/jazzguitartranscriptions
- https://www.instagram.com/panzerschwein

PayPal: elexandor@gmx.net // BUSD (BEP20): 0xEd979ad7E9d7E3f6f7cB7c2830aA2ae1DfBB1A6D

panzerschwein@gmx.de // Cologne, Germany

Feb 2022

~ Table Of Contents ~

~ C harmonic major ~

2

3

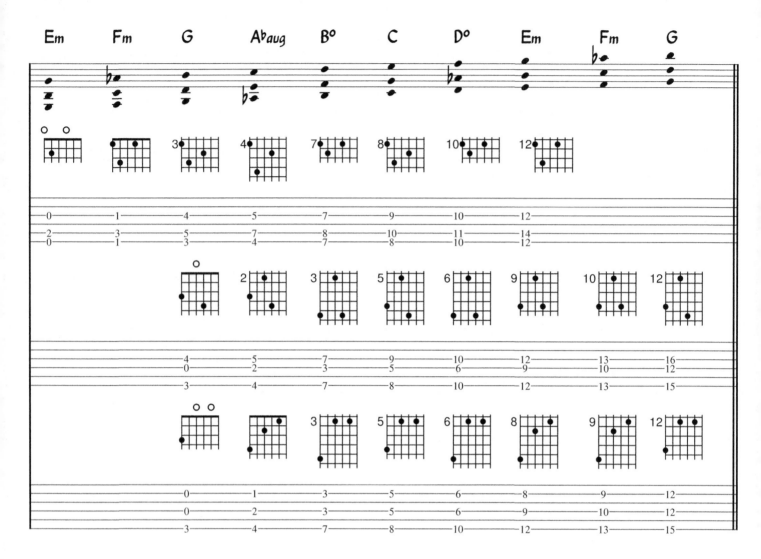

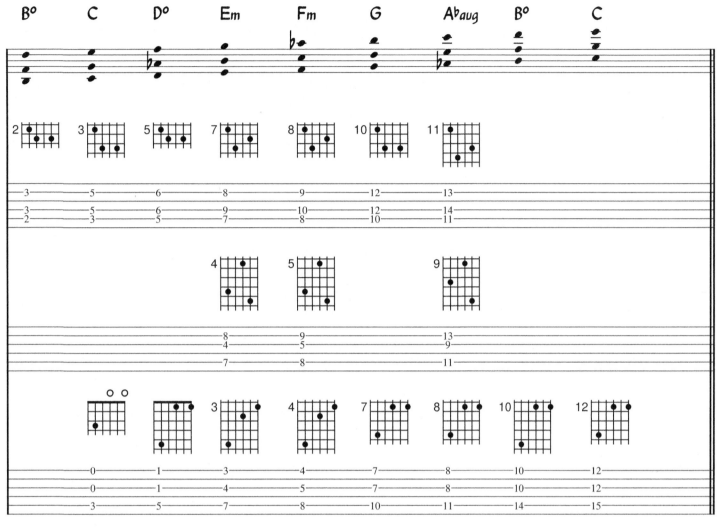

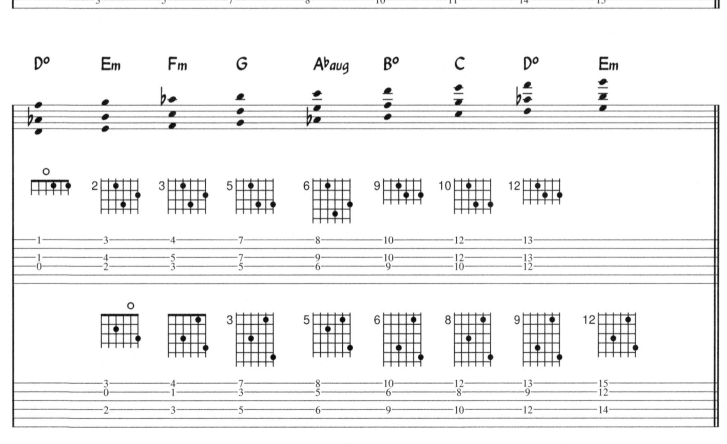

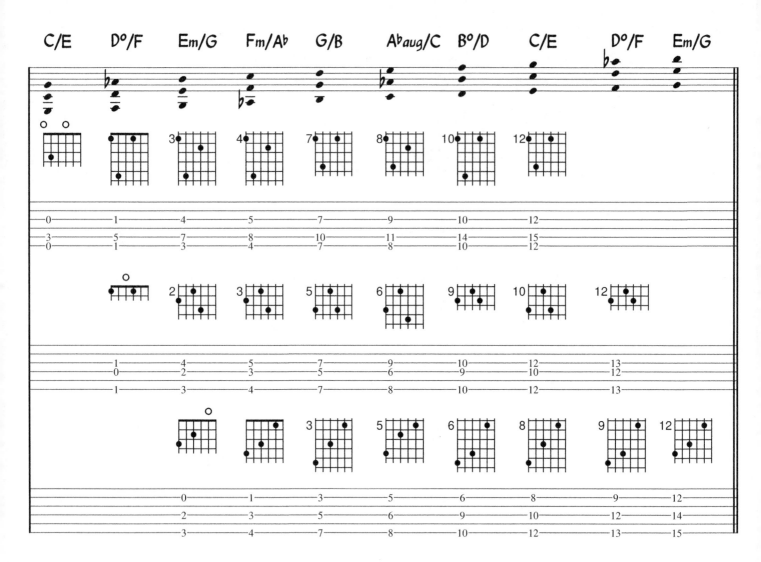

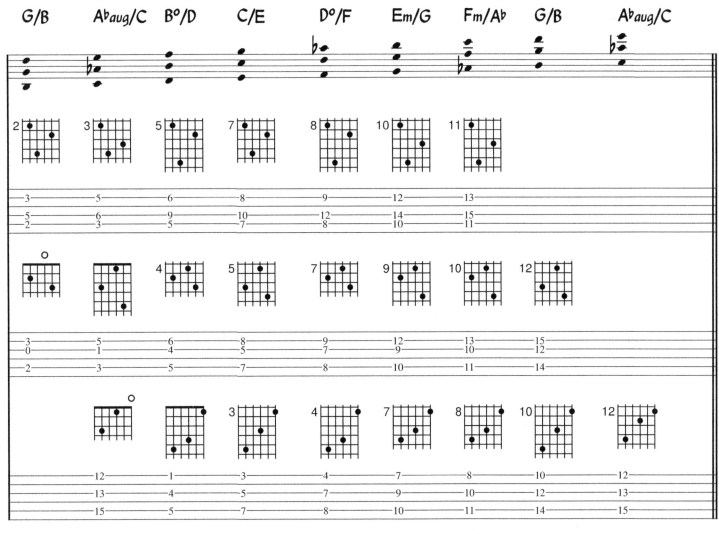

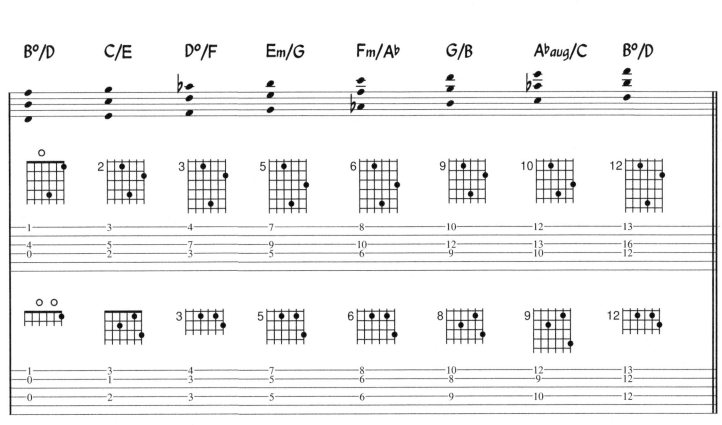

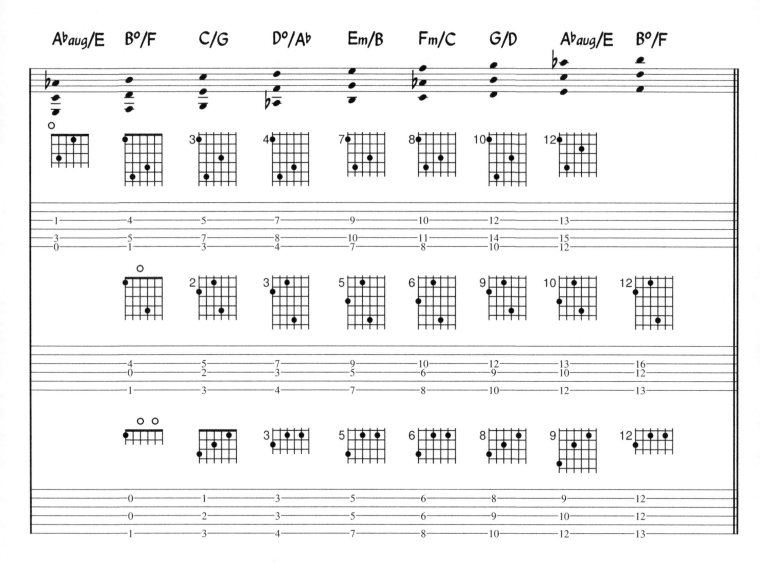

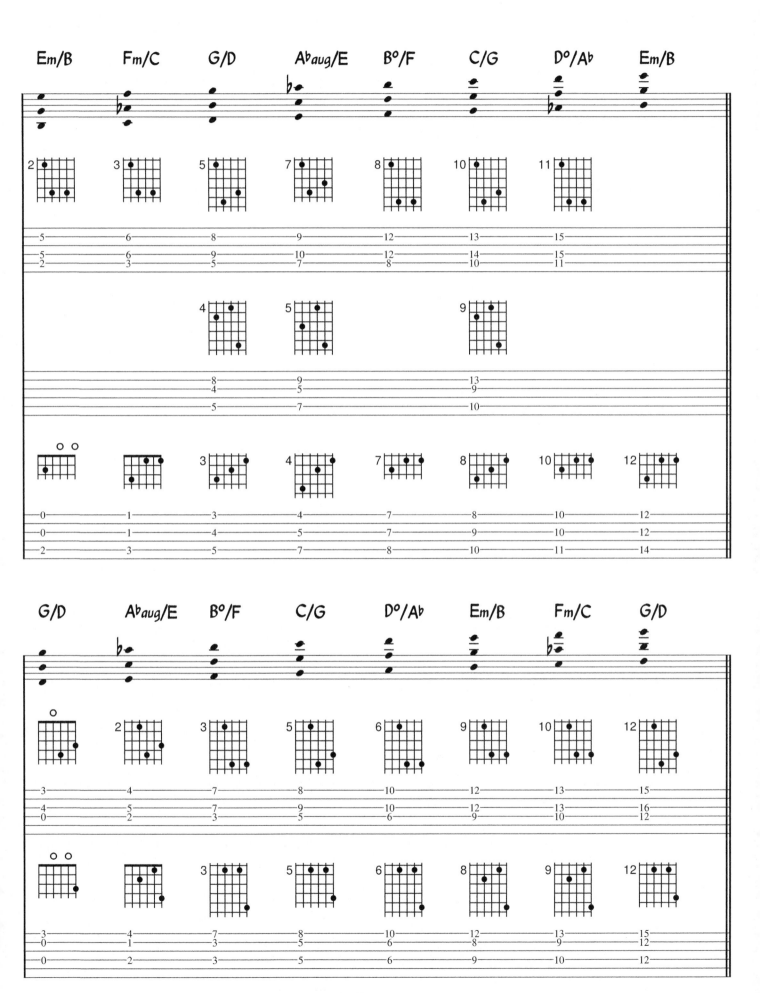

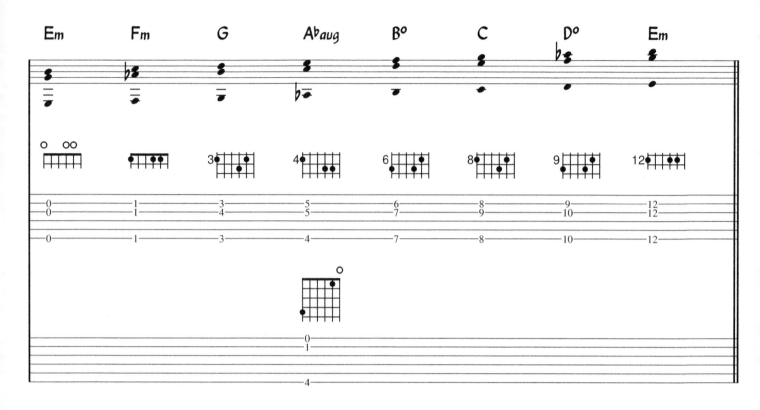

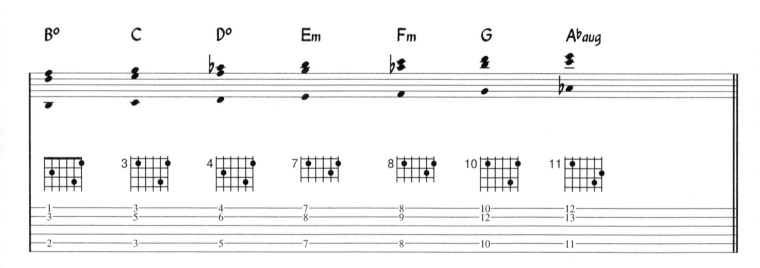

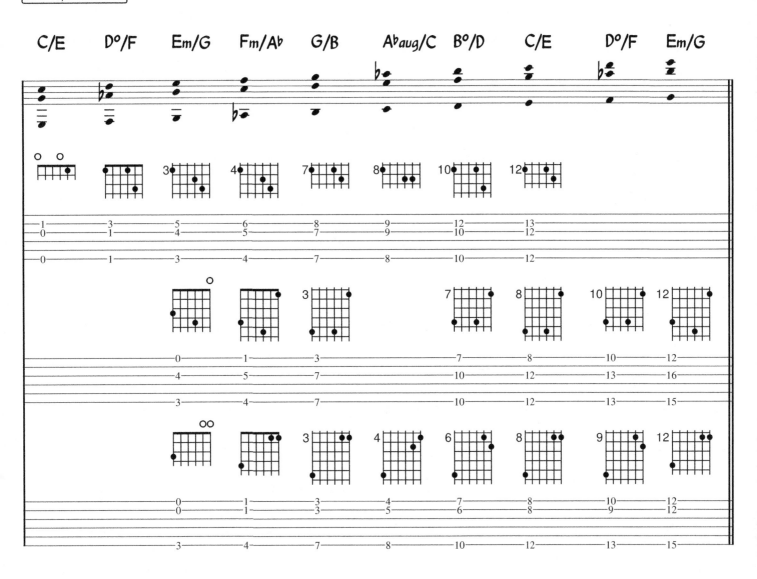

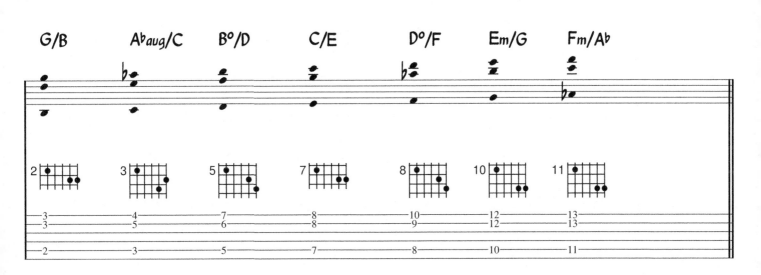

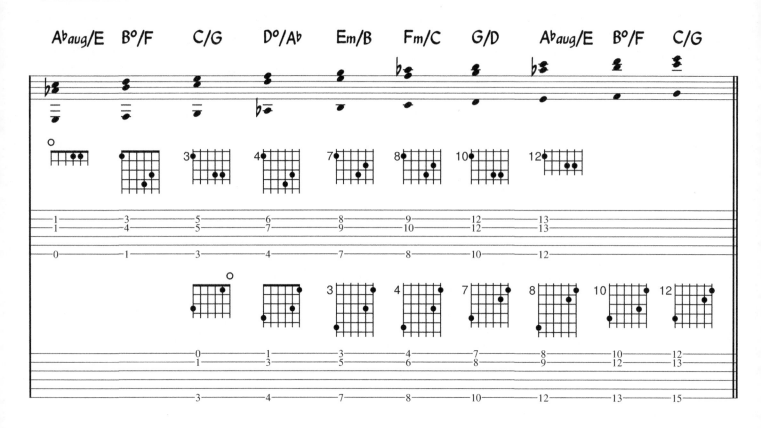

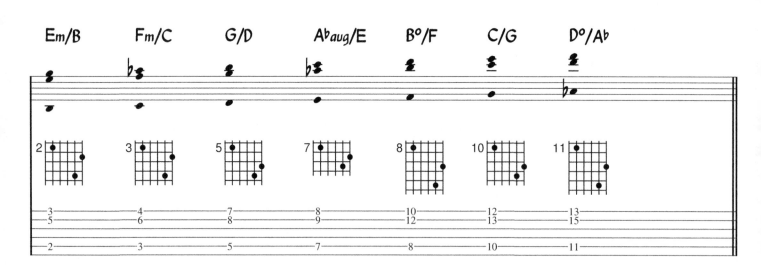

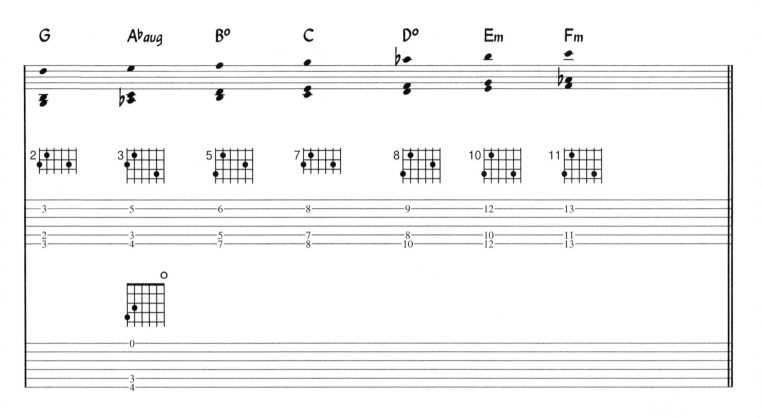

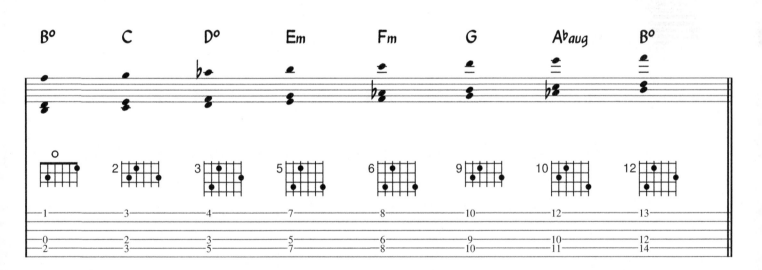

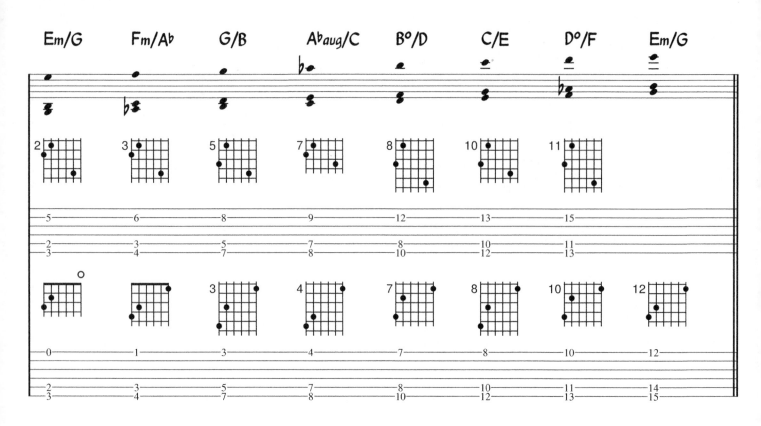

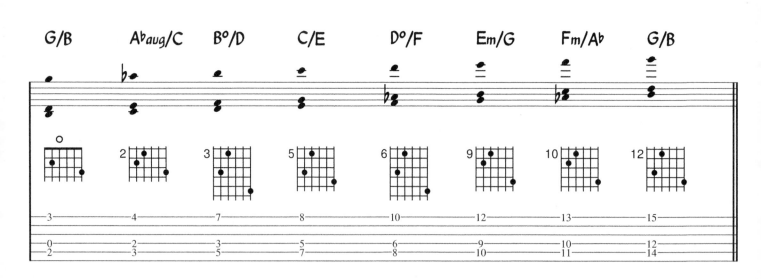

14

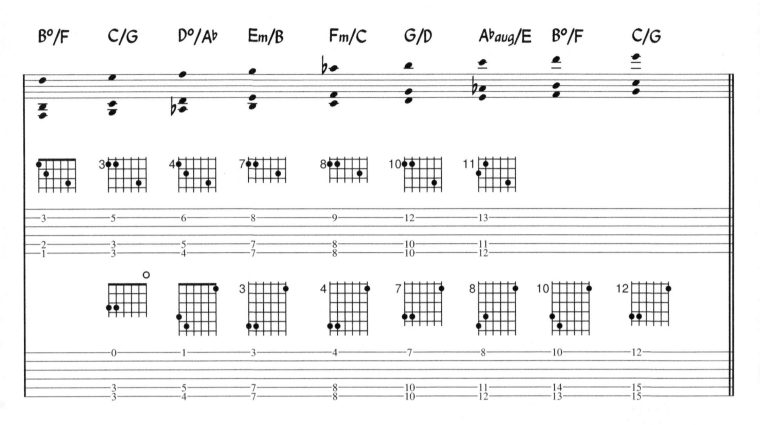

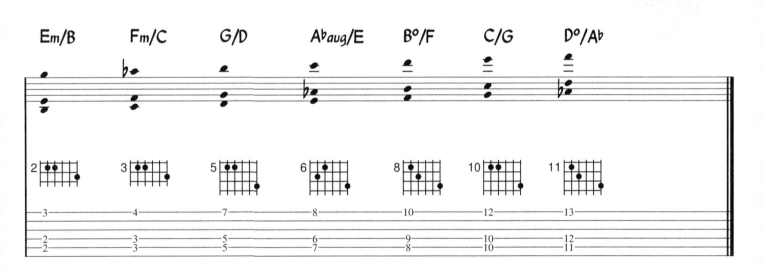

~ G harmonic major ~

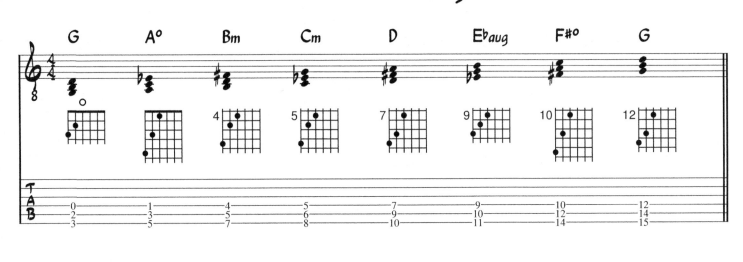

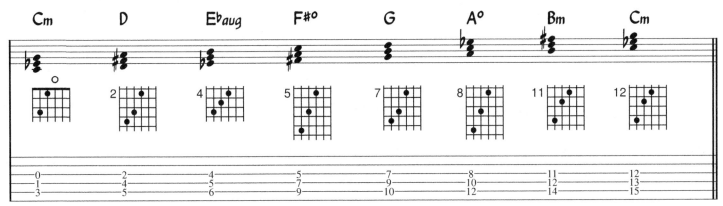

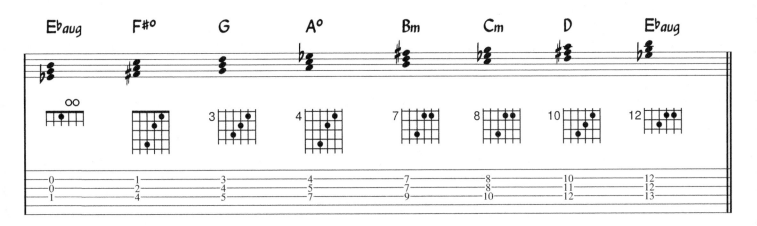

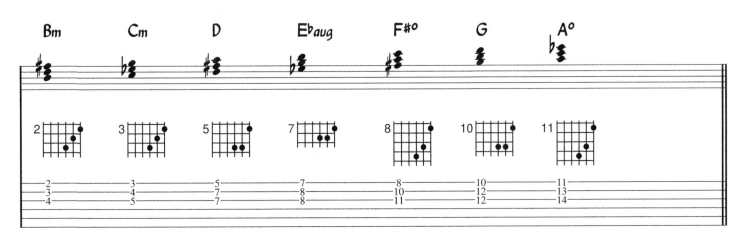

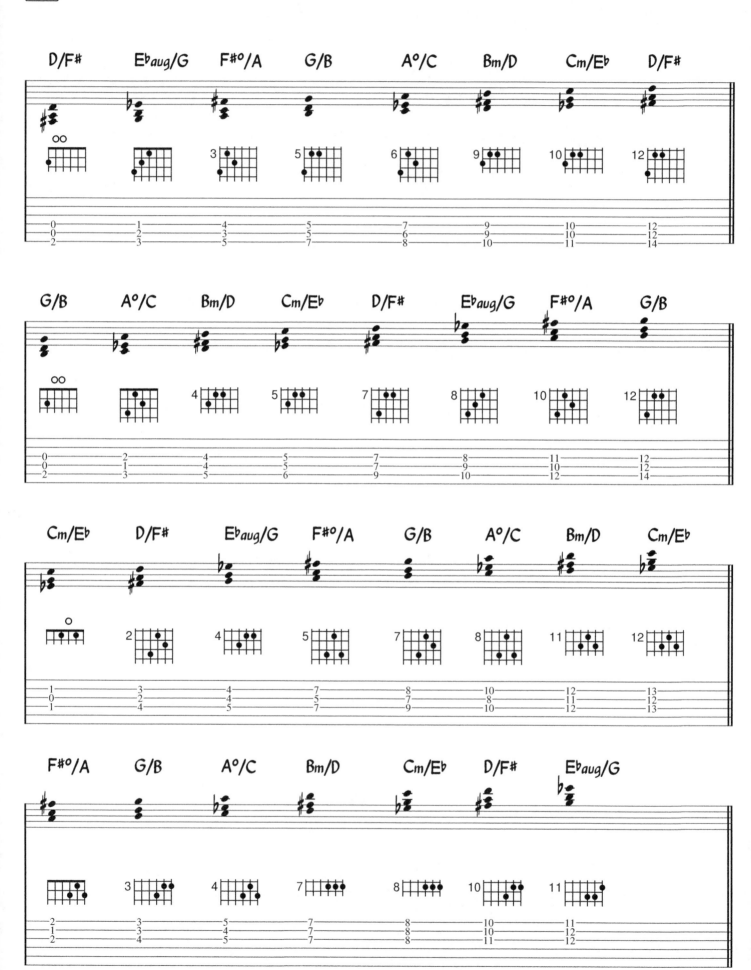

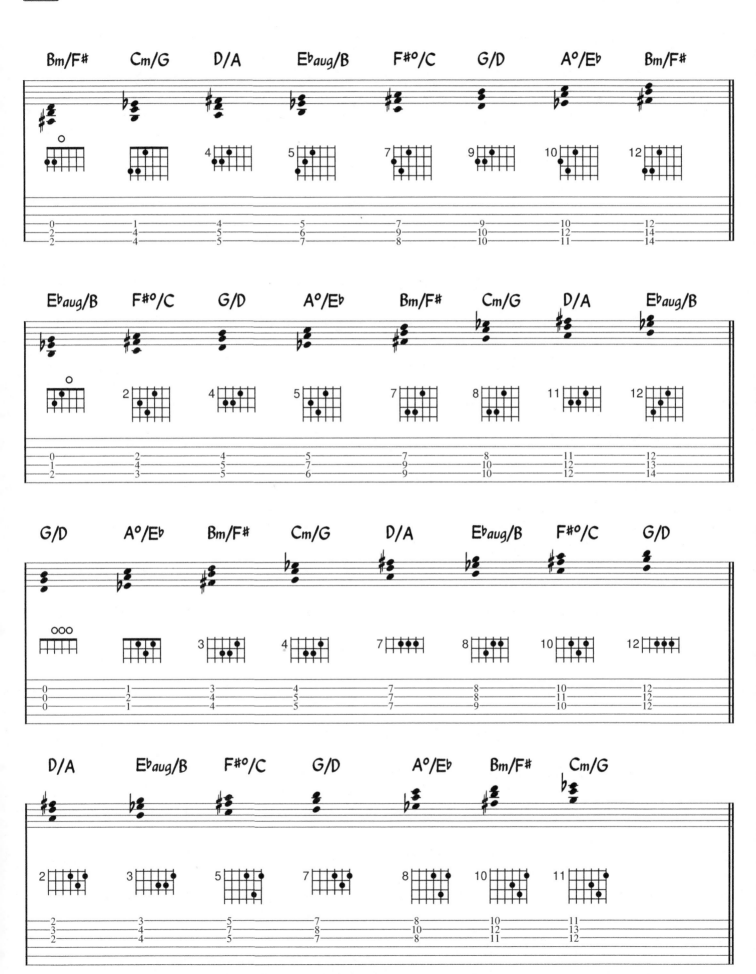

19

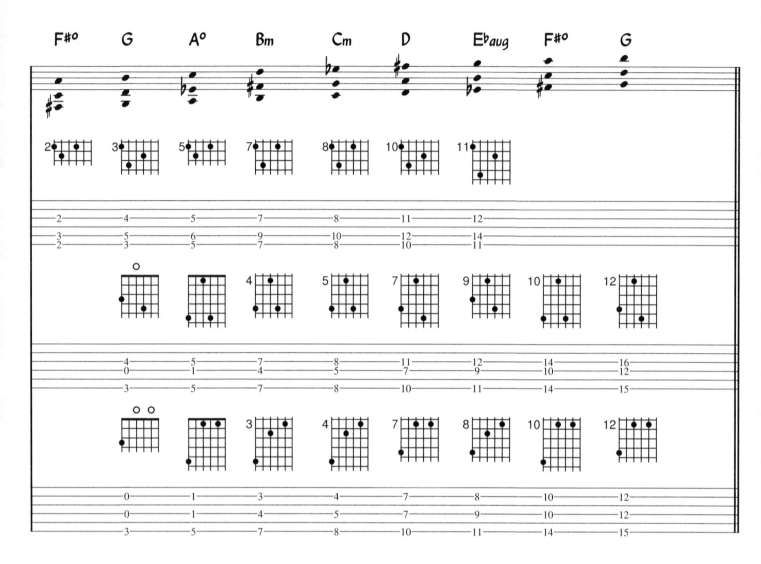

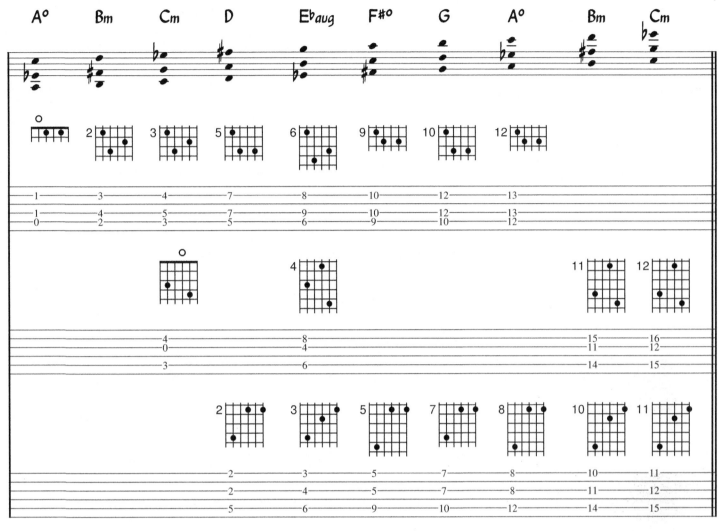

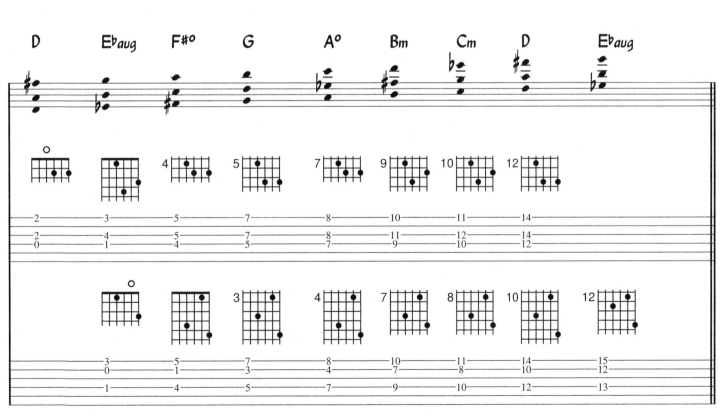

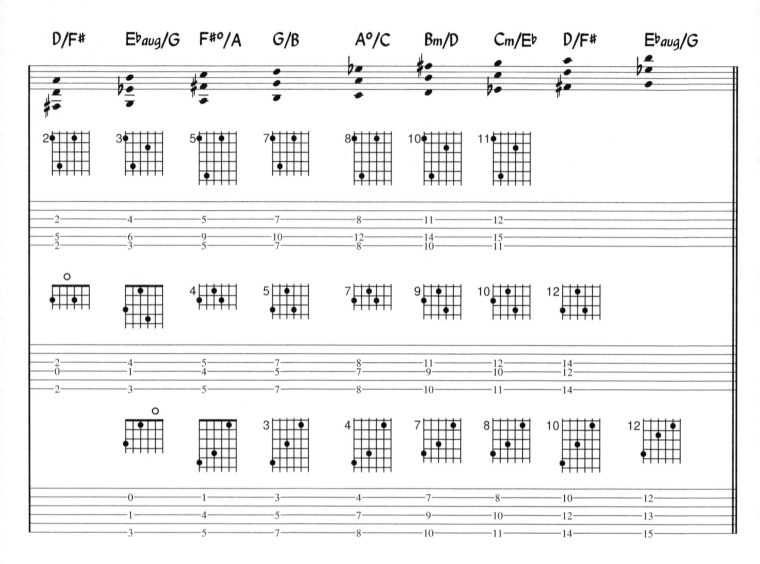

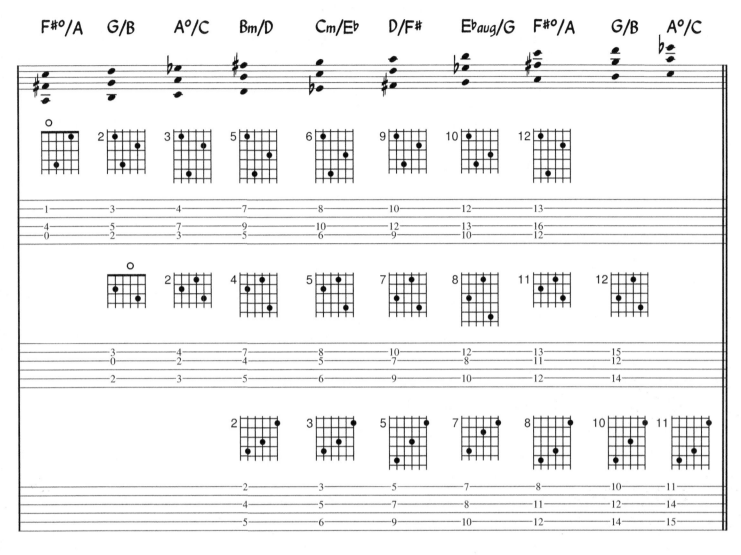

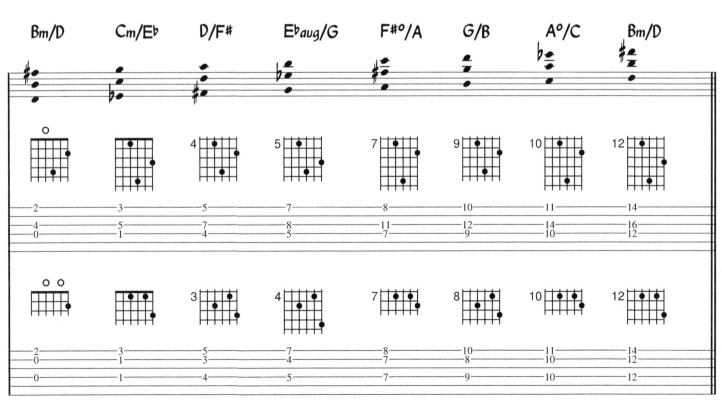

23

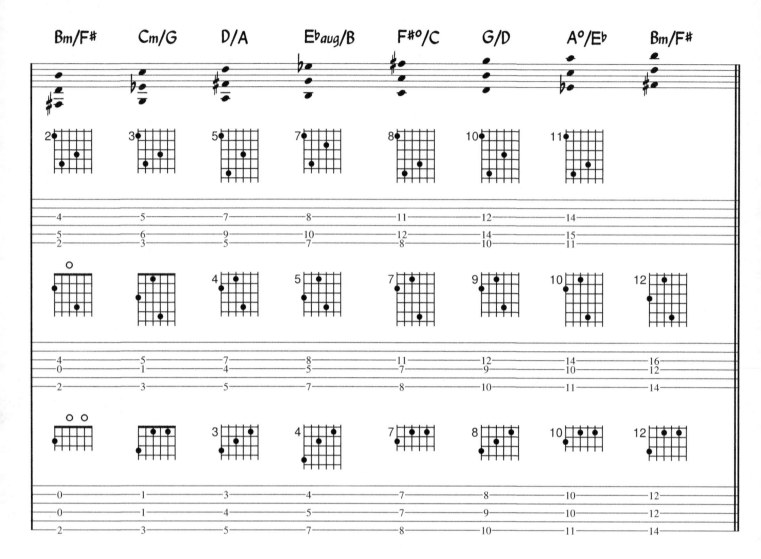

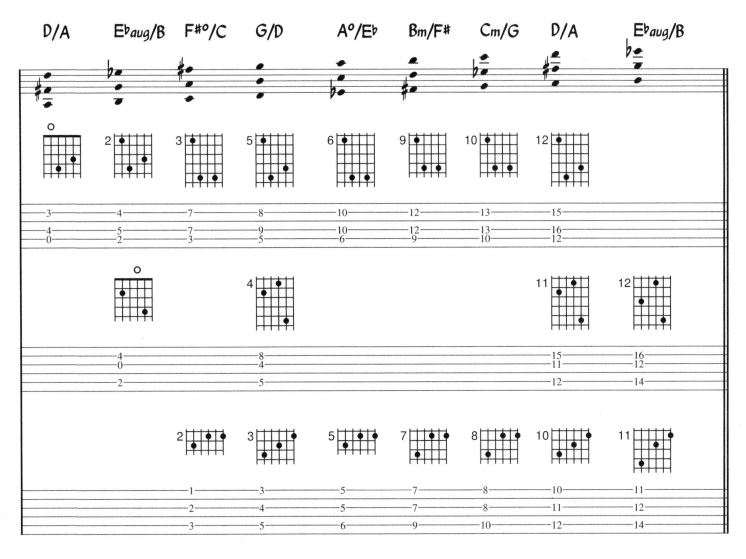

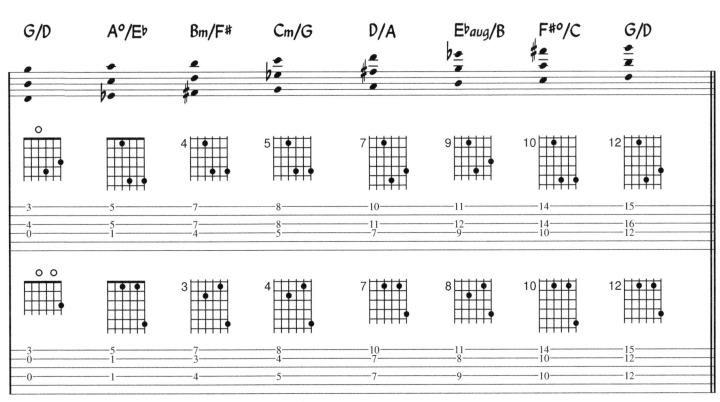

25

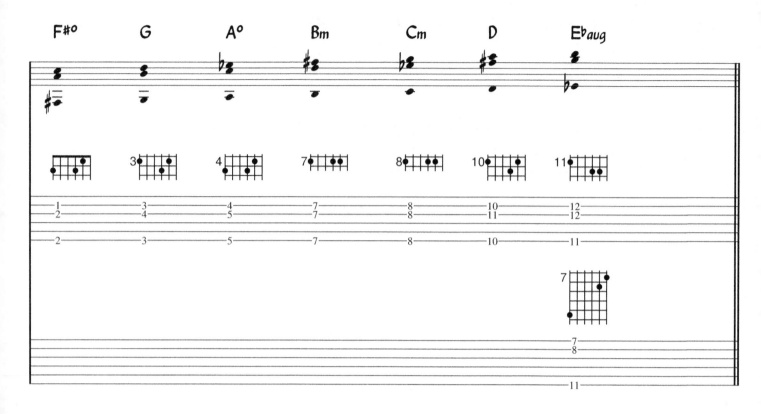

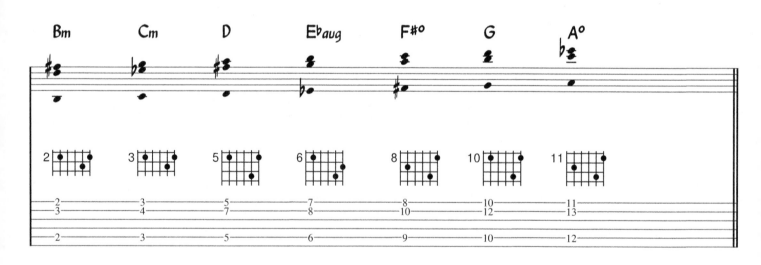

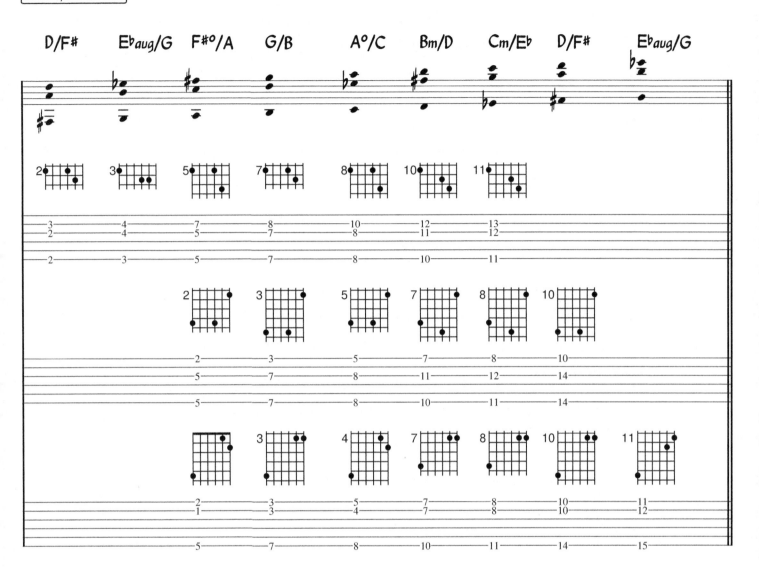

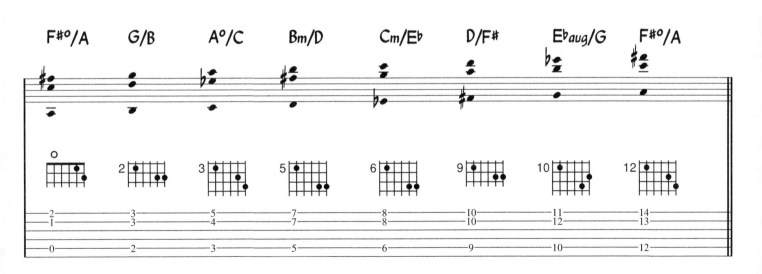

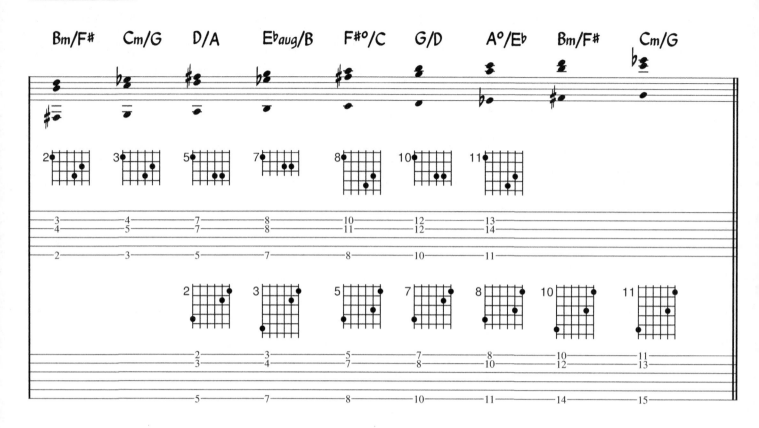

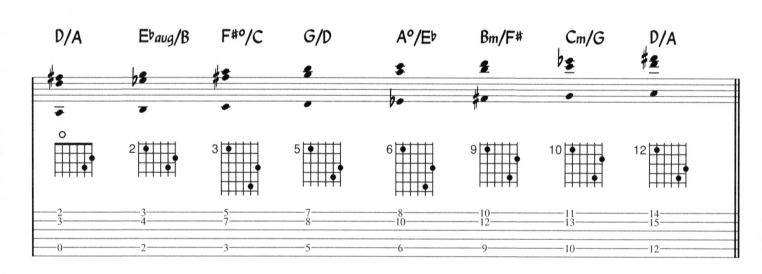

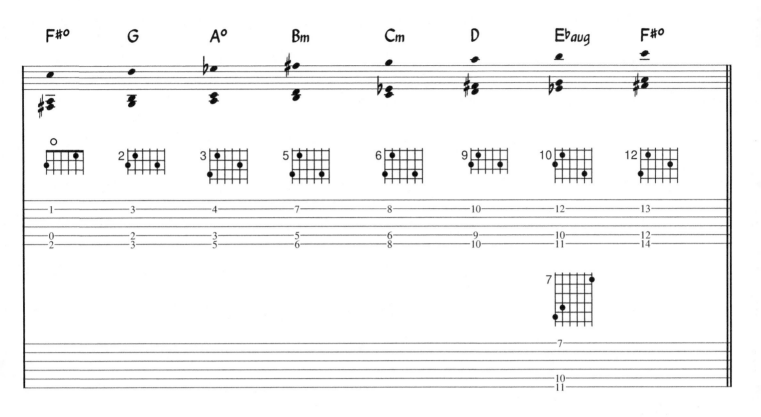

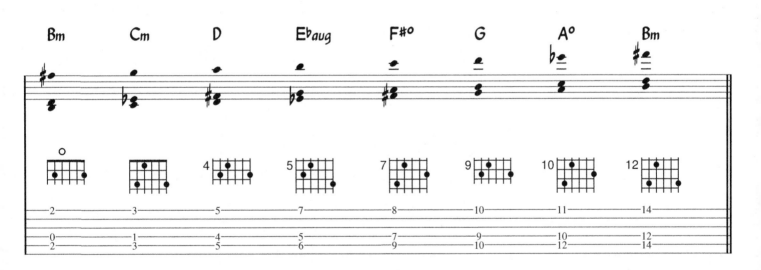

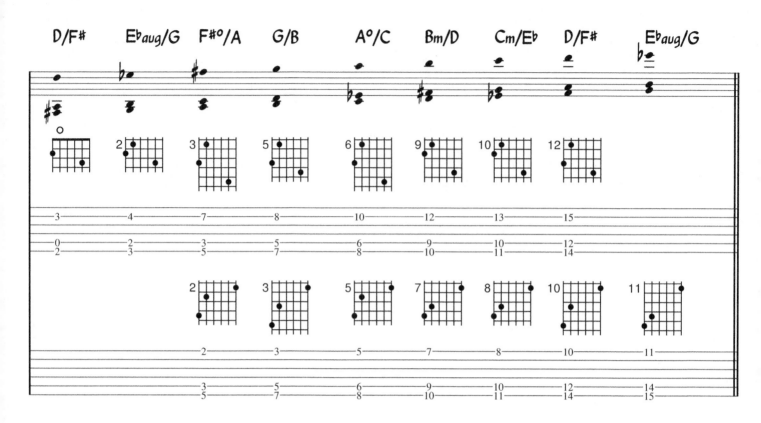

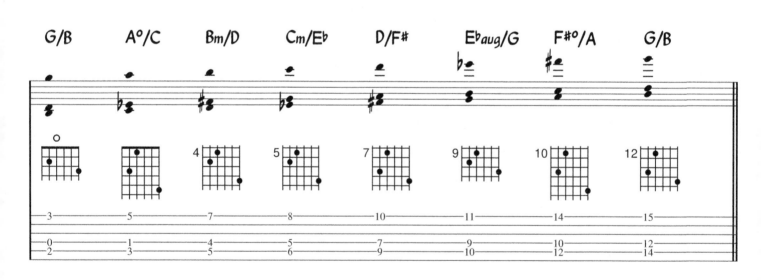

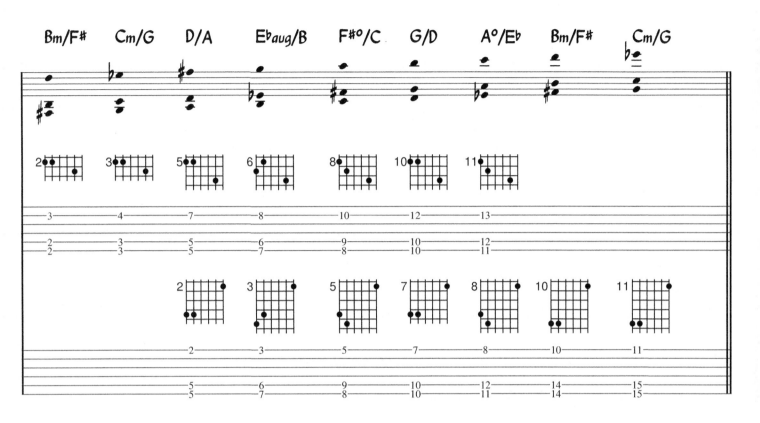

Bm/F#   Cm/G   D/A   Ebaug/B   F#o/C   G/D   Ao/Eb   Bm/F#   Cm/G

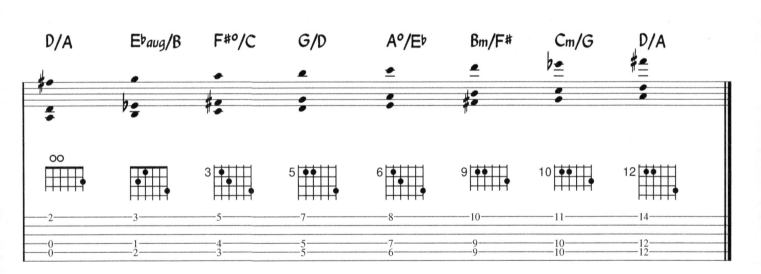

D/A   Ebaug/B   F#o/C   G/D   Ao/Eb   Bm/F#   Cm/G   D/A

31

~ D harmonic major ~

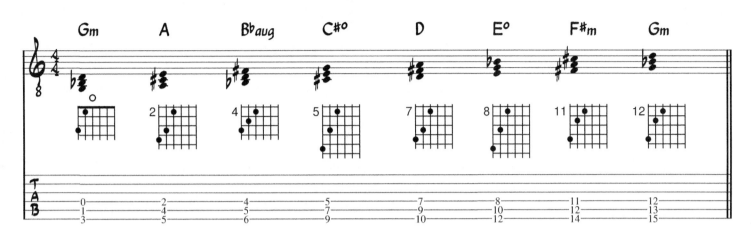

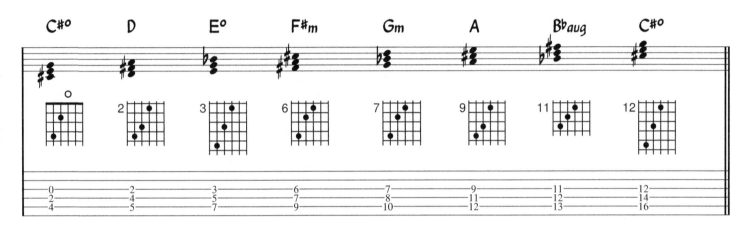

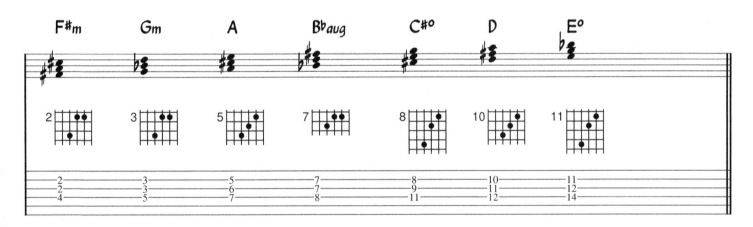

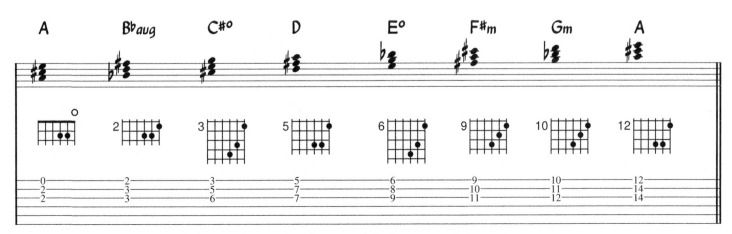

34

35

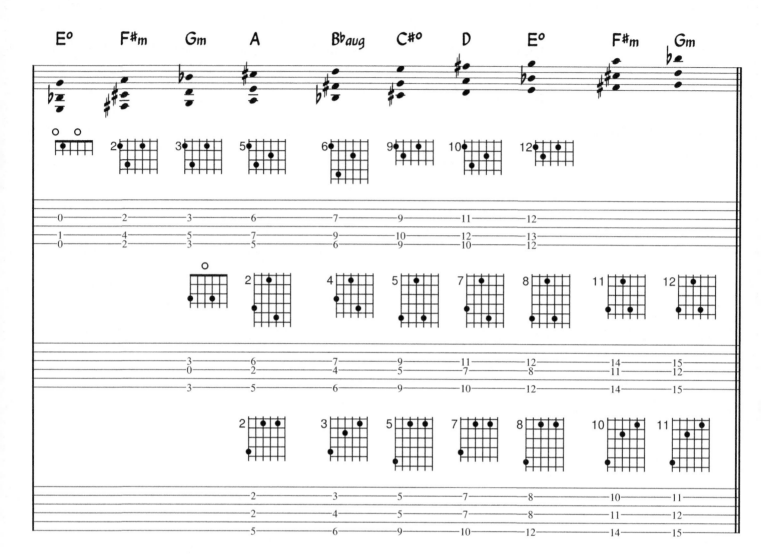

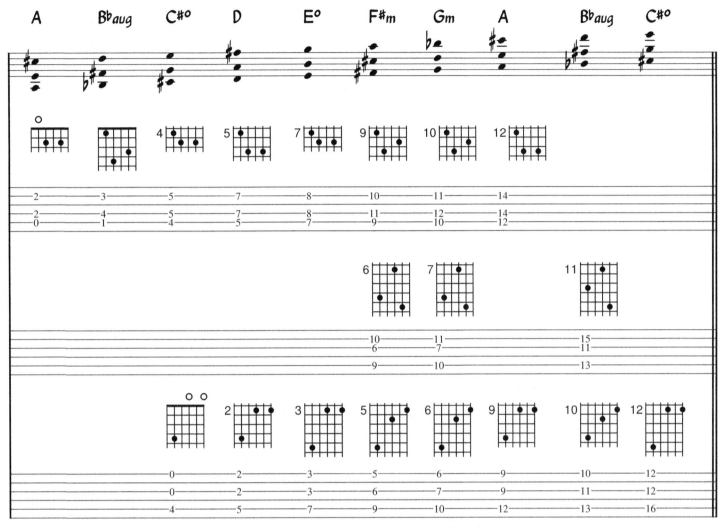

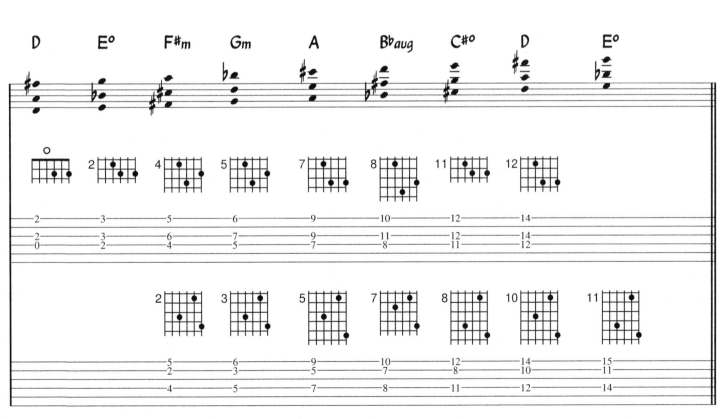

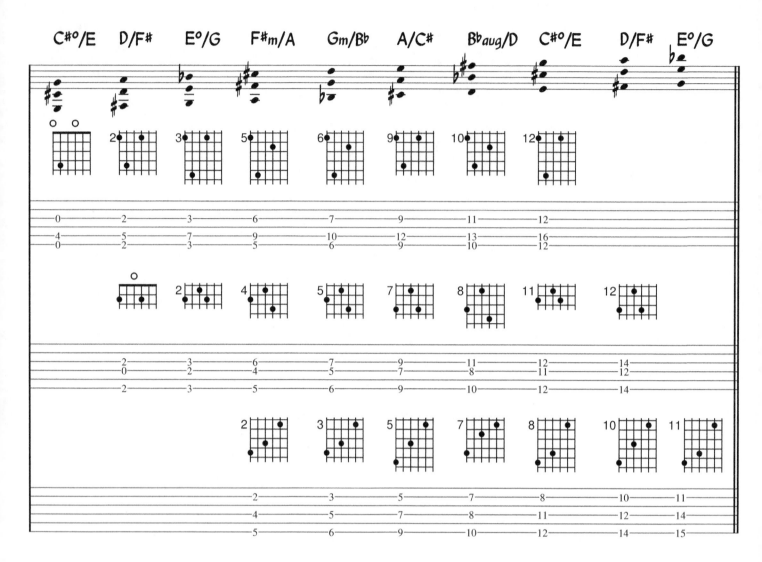

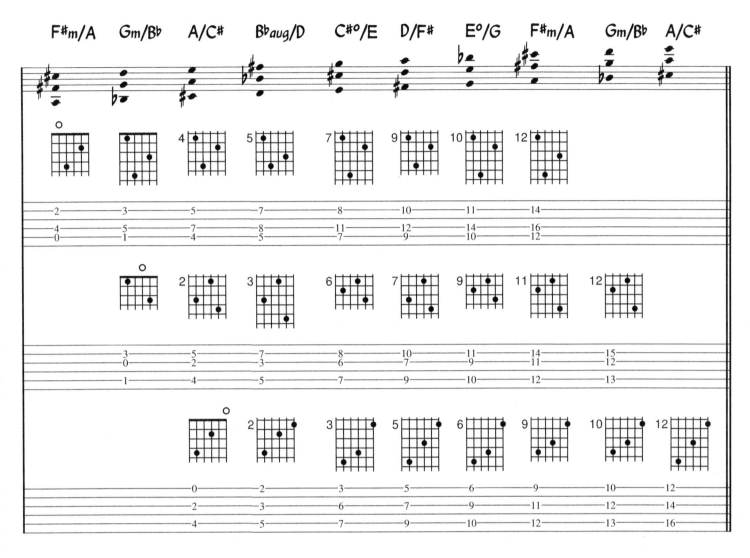

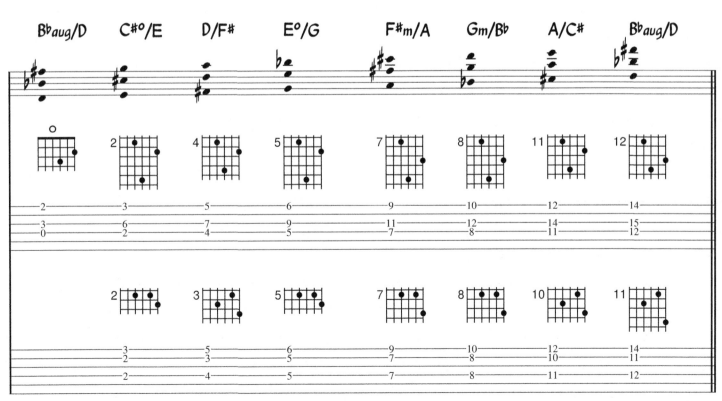

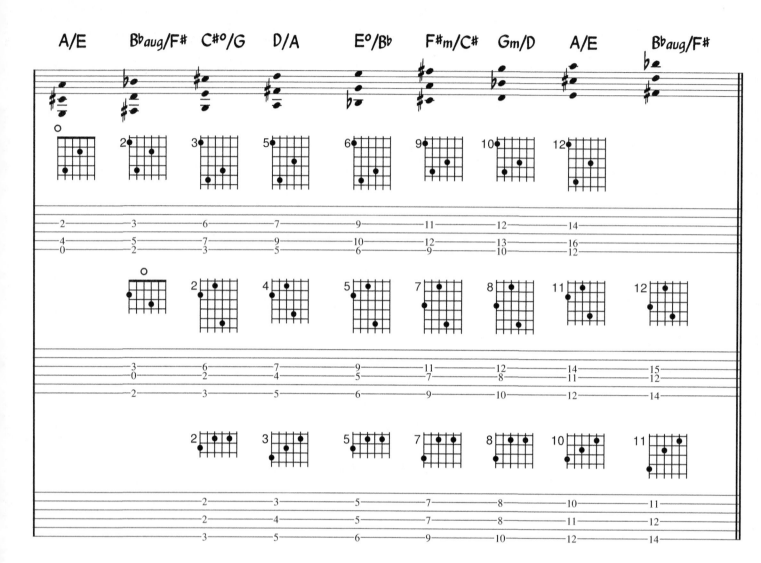

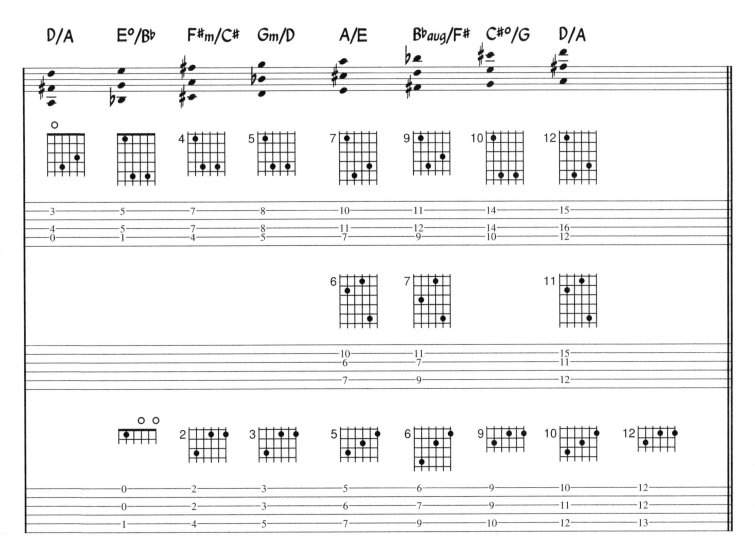

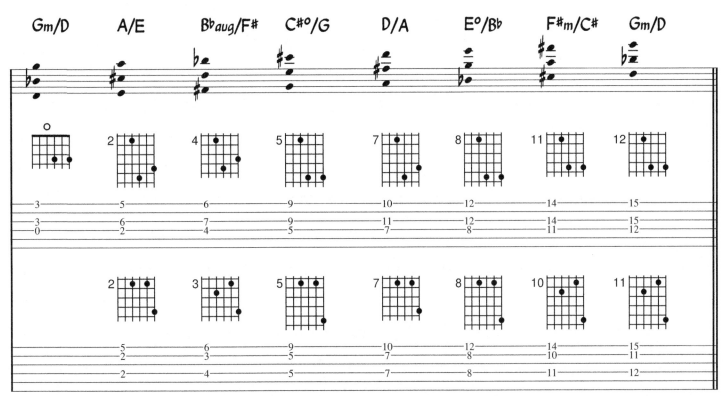

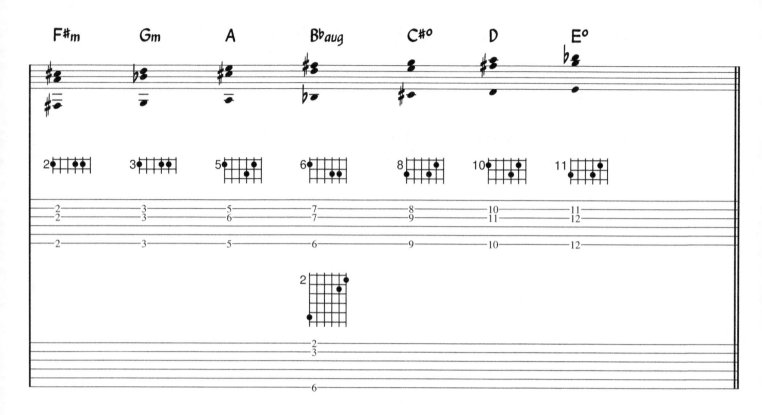

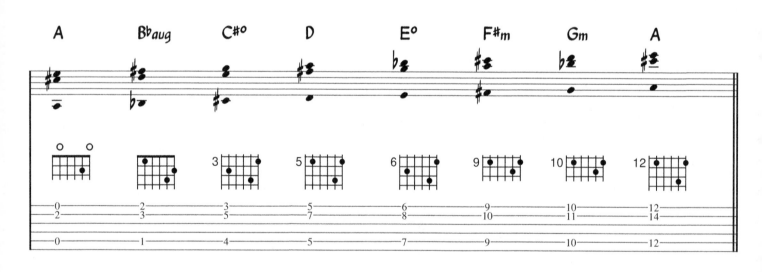

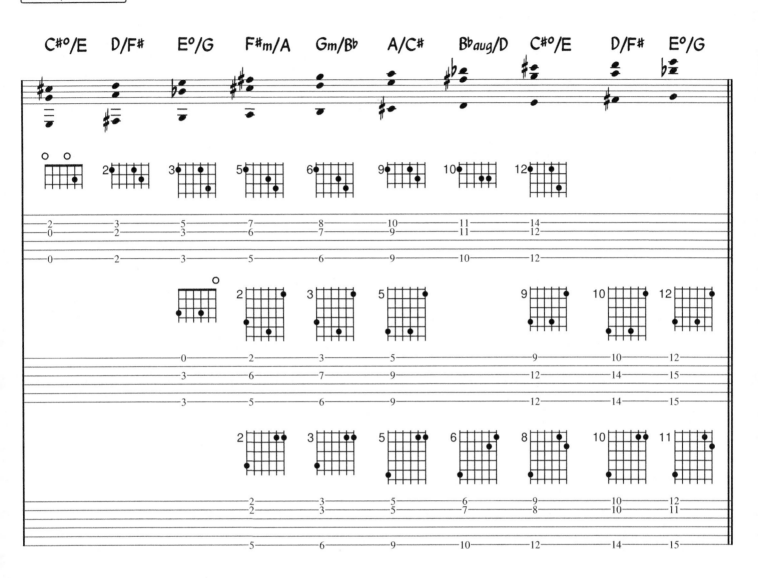

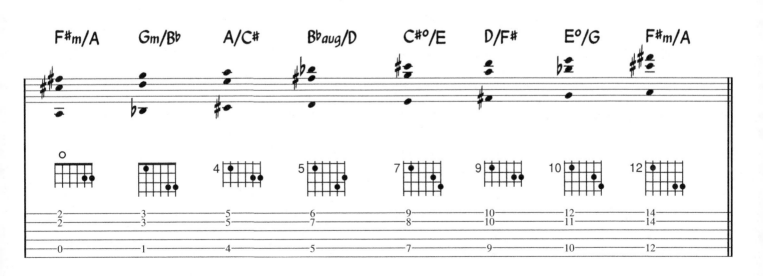

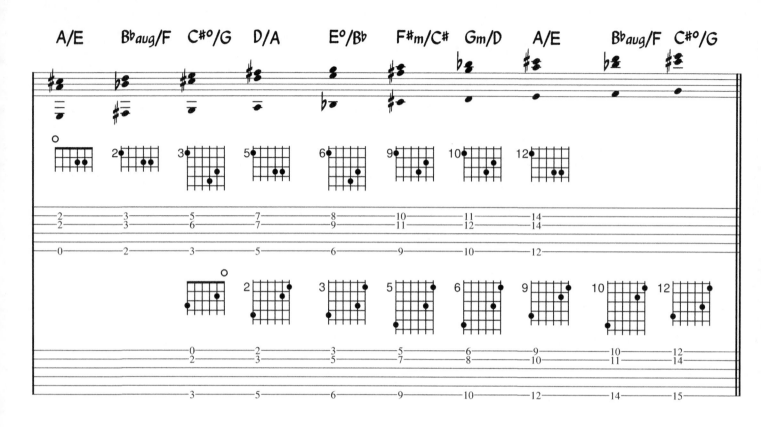

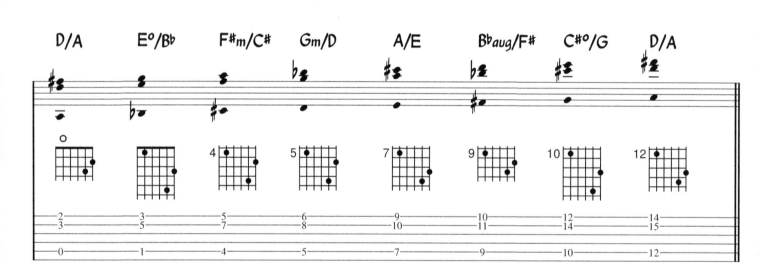

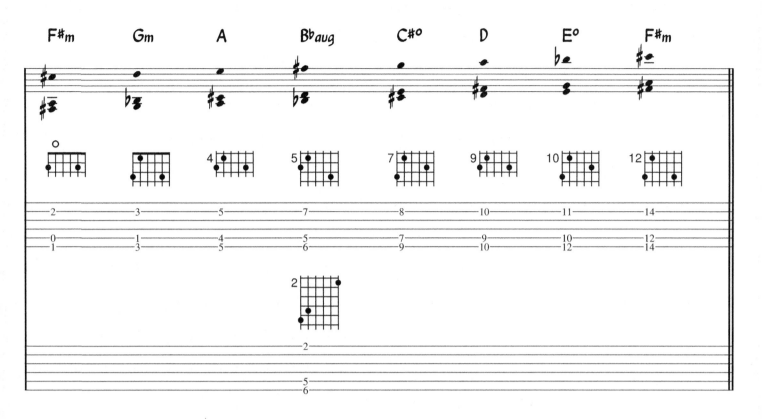

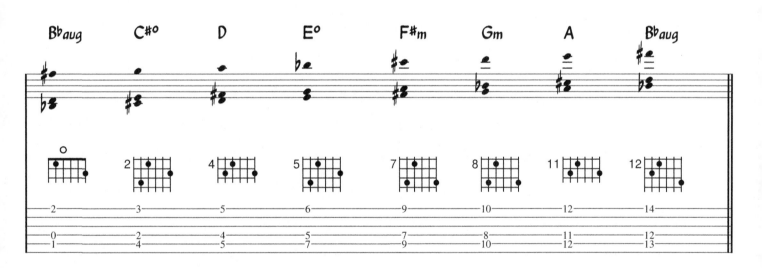

45

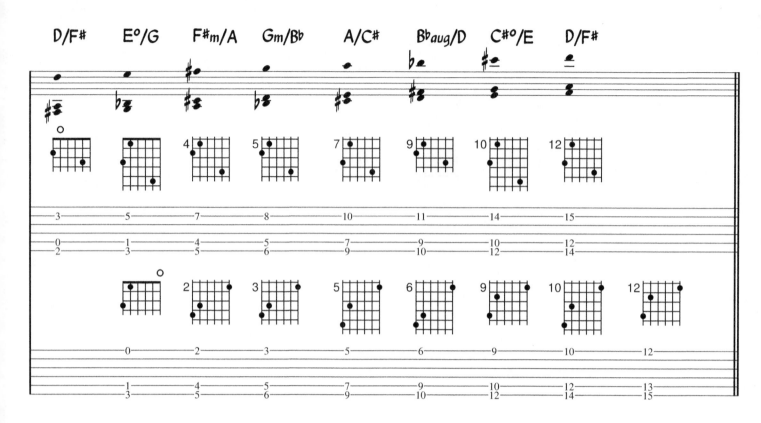

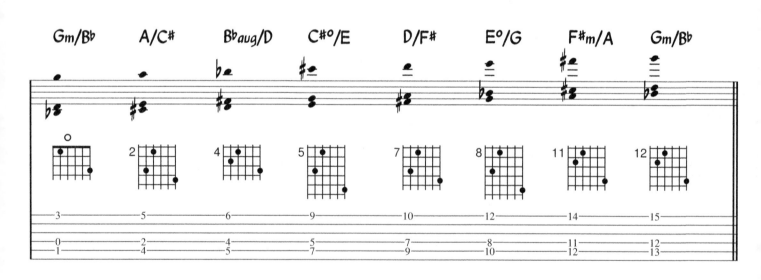

46

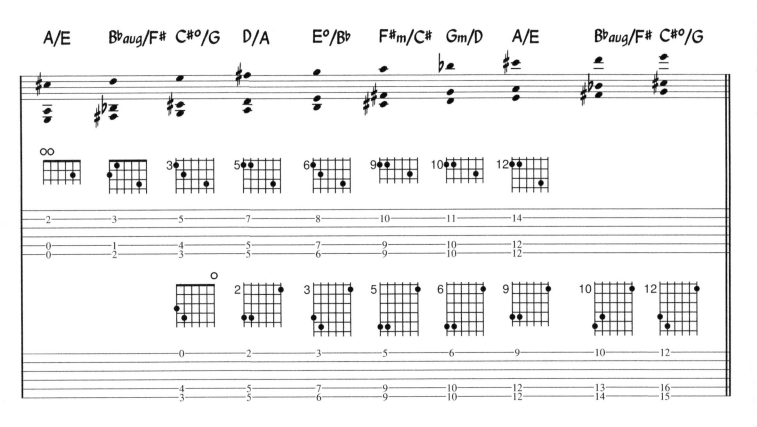

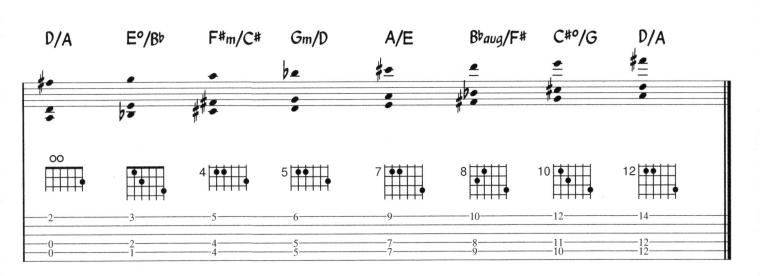

~ A harmonic major ~

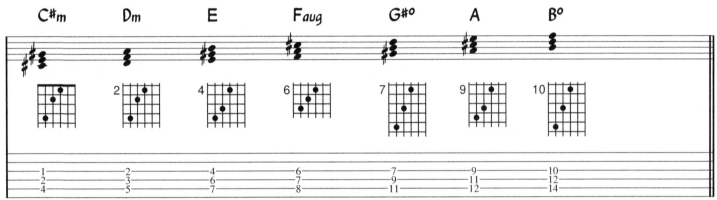

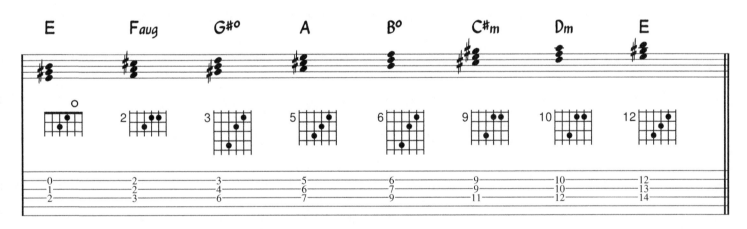

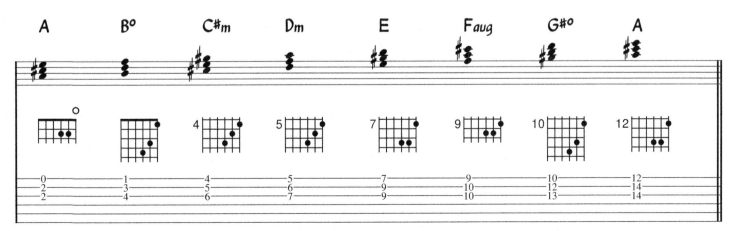

50

51

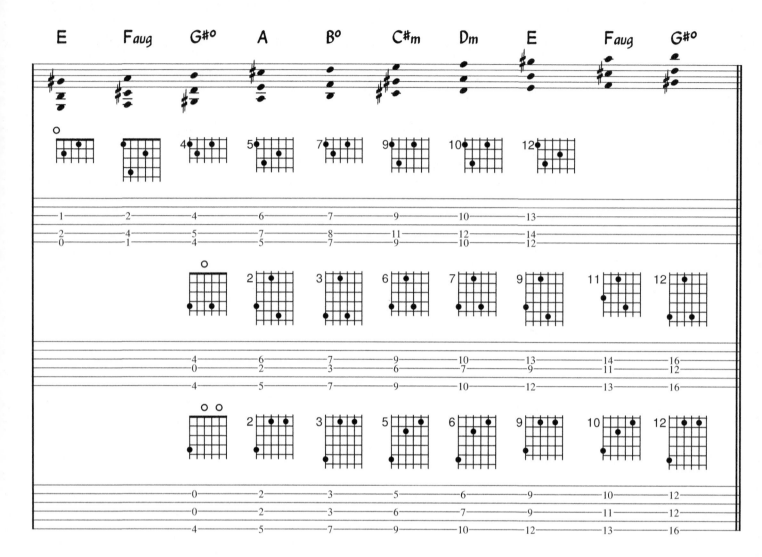

52

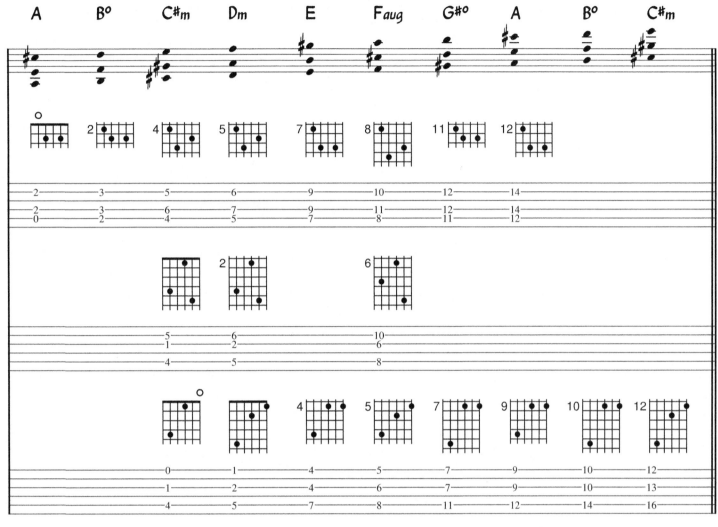

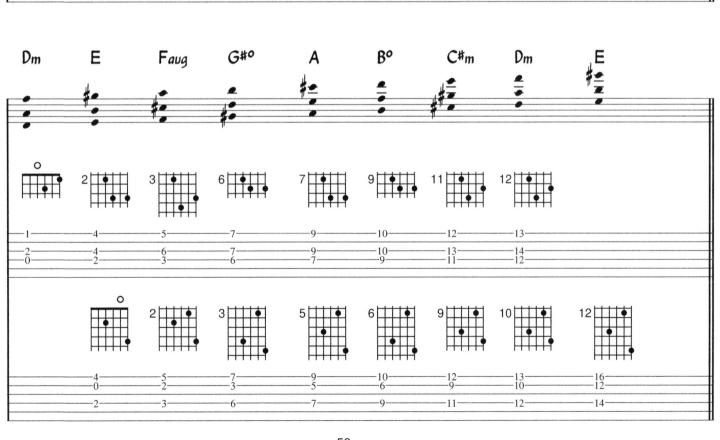

53

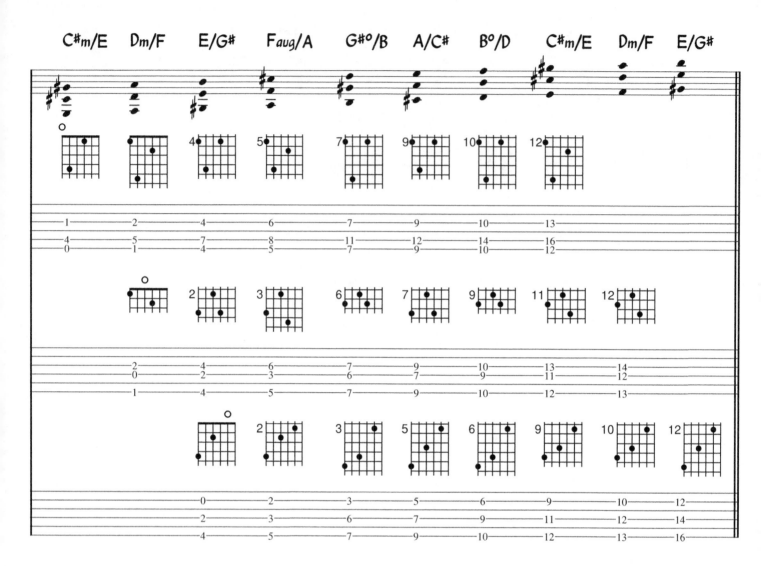

54

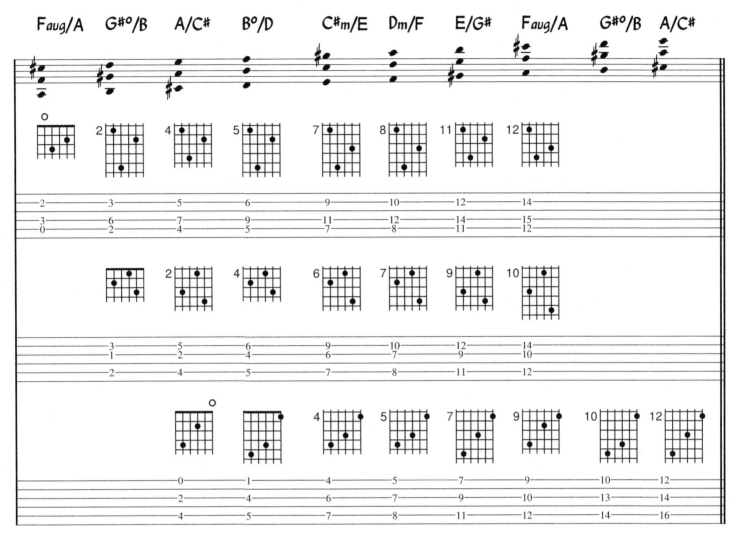

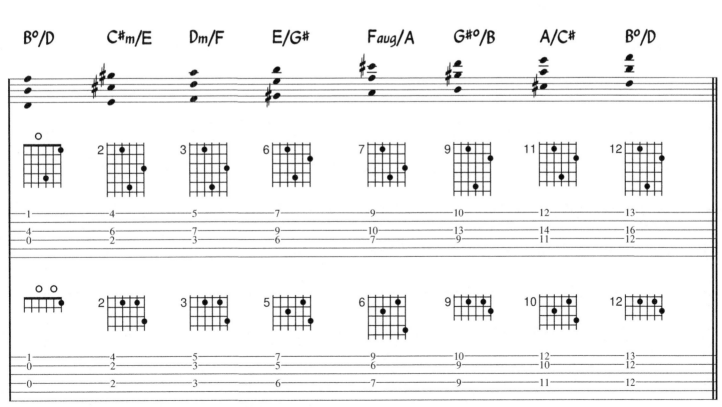

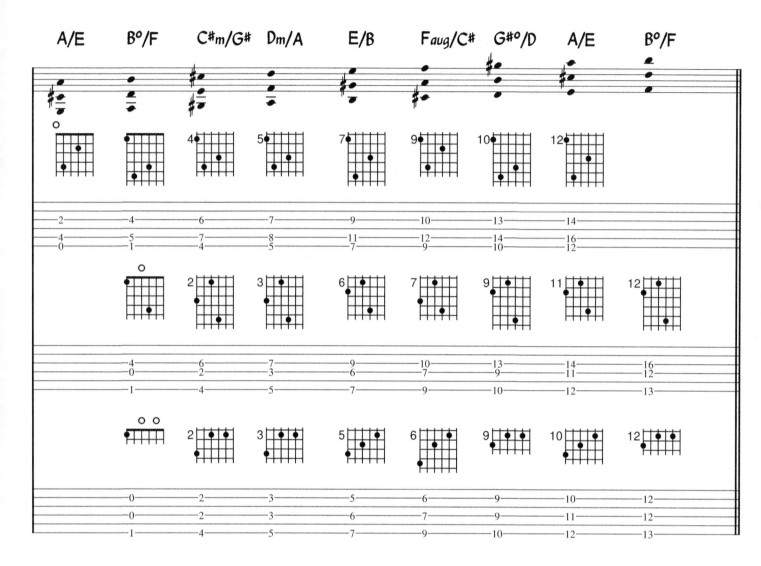

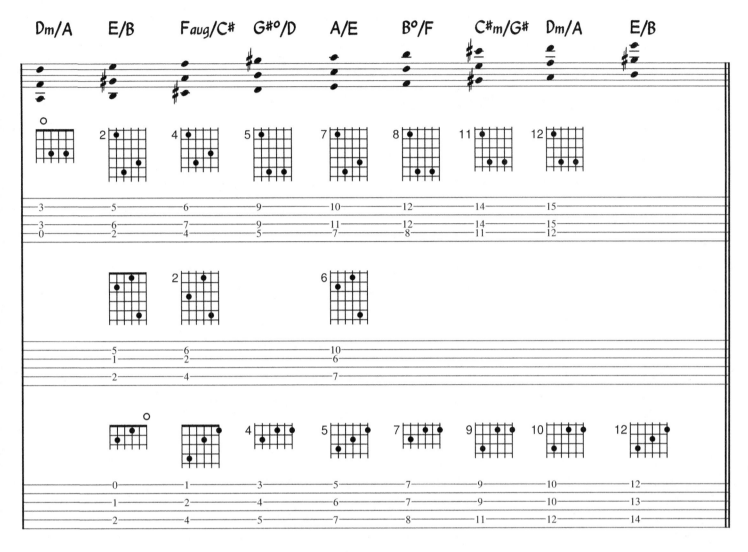

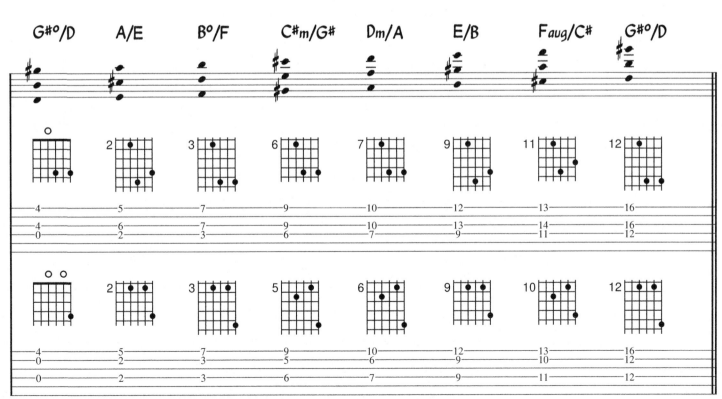

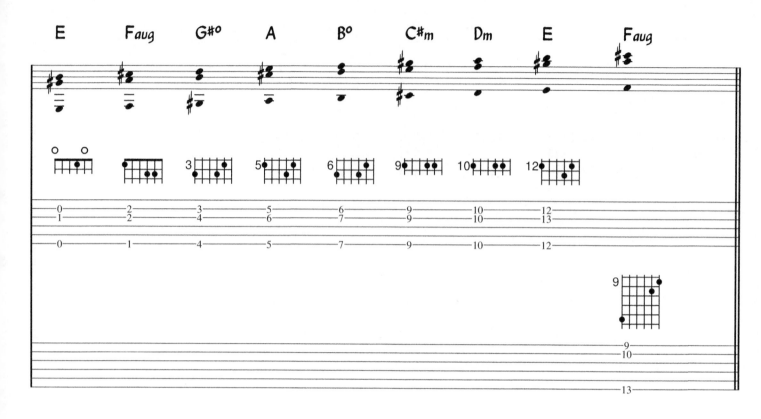

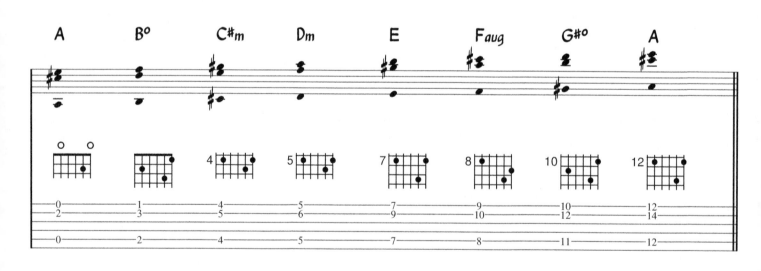

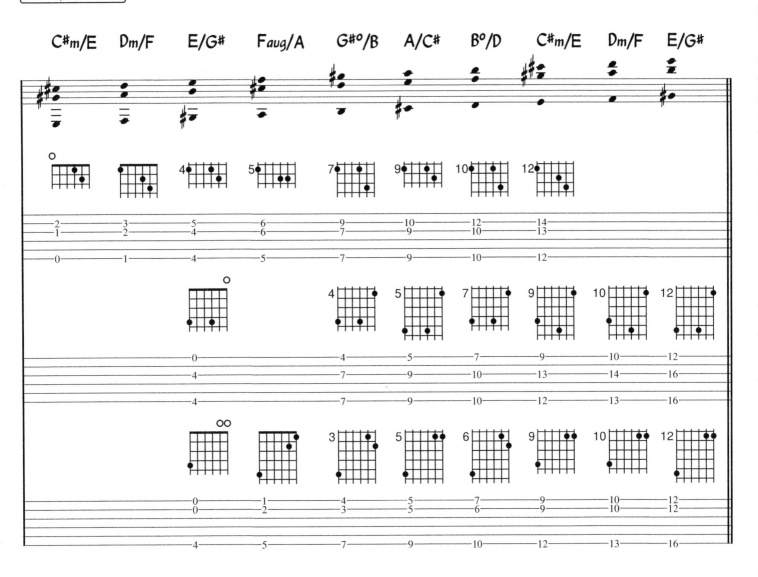

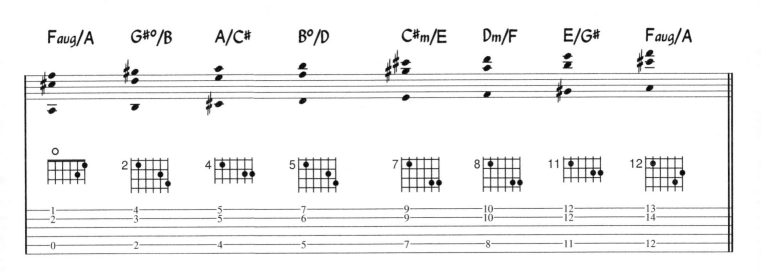

59

2nd inv. (open voiced, Version 2)

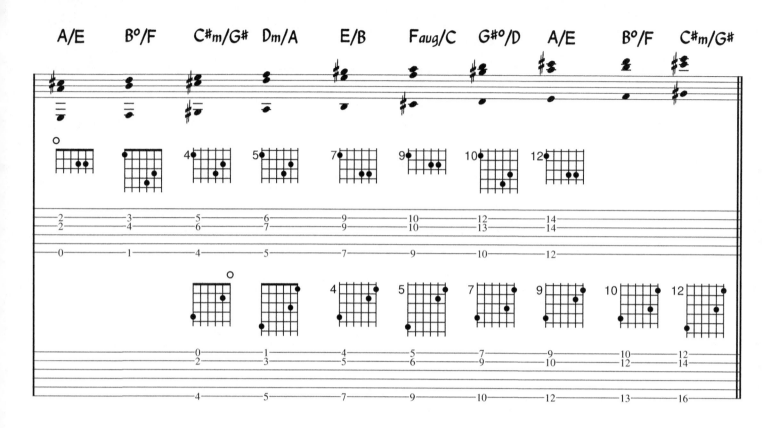

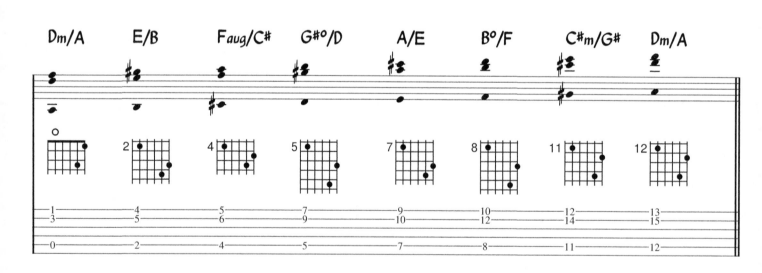

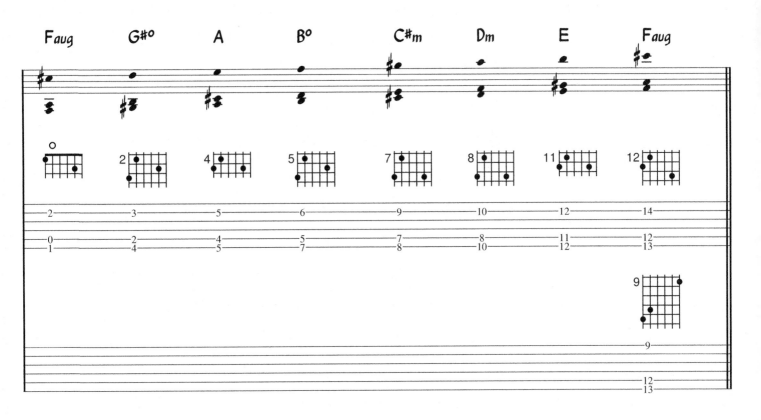

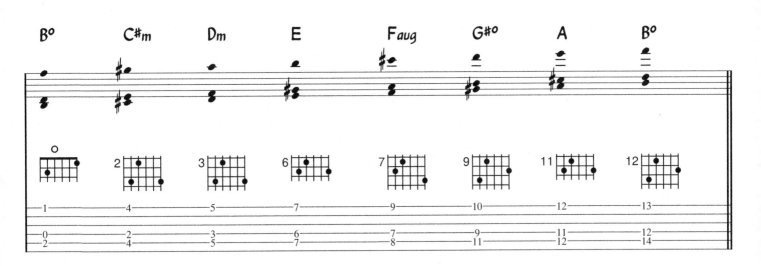

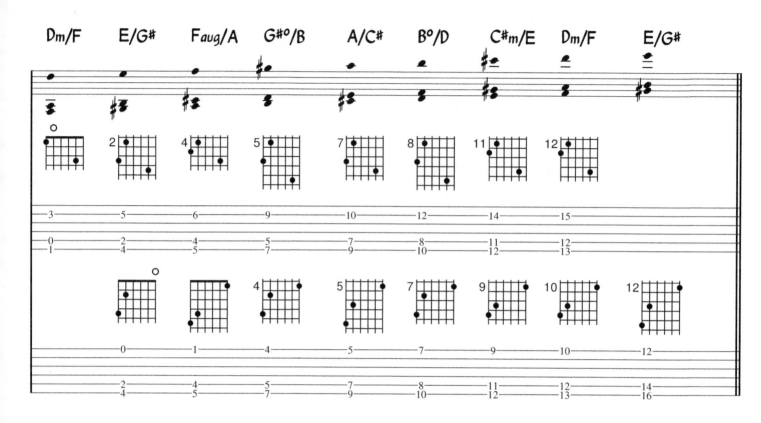

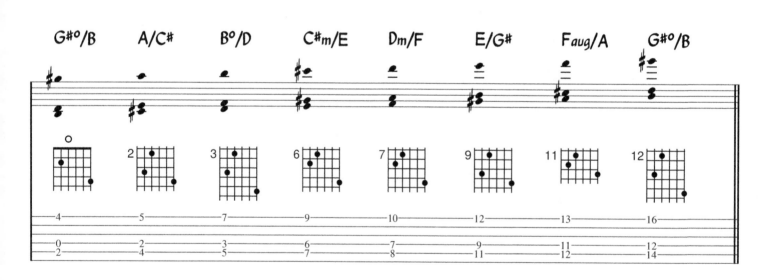

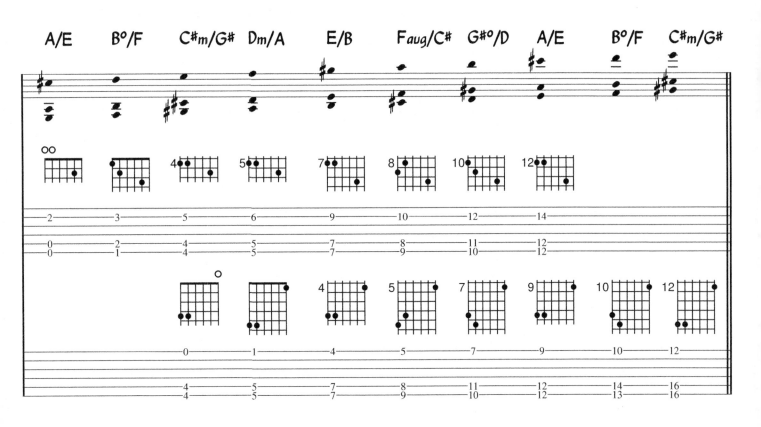

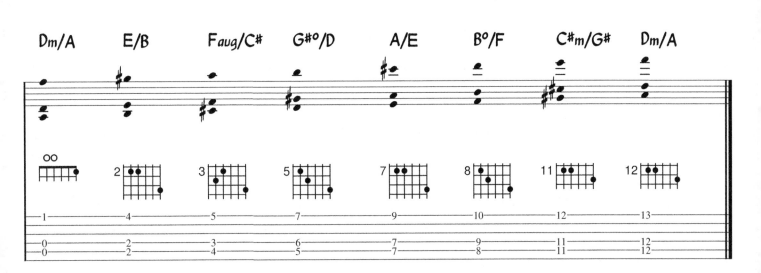

63

~ E harmonic major ~

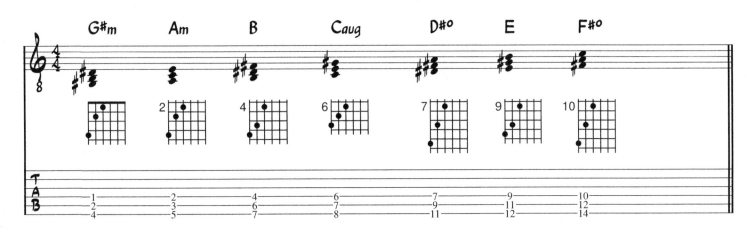

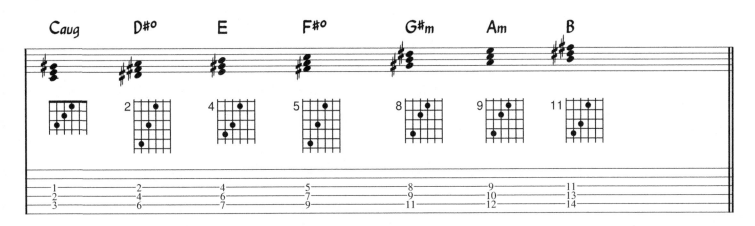

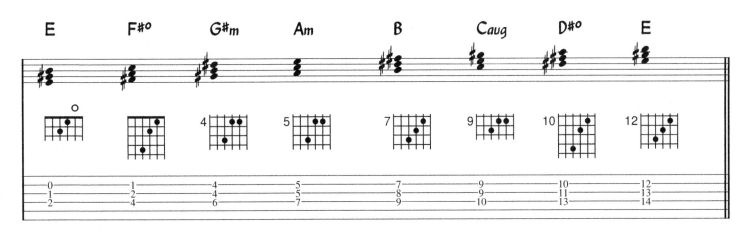

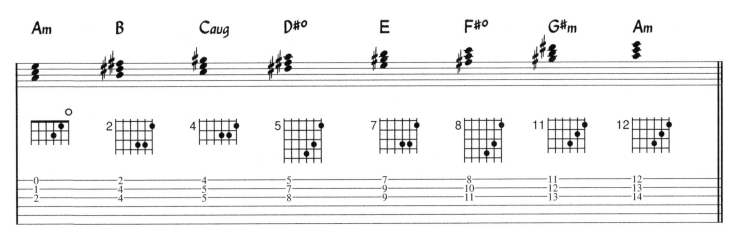

67

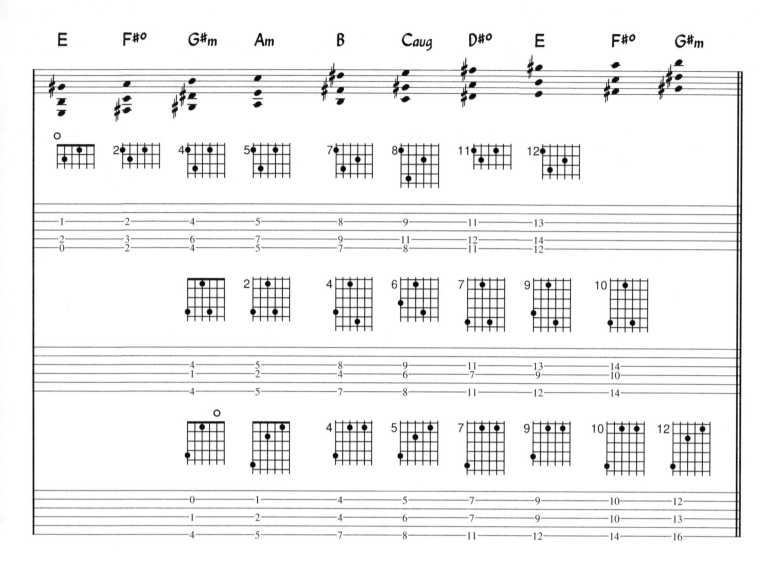

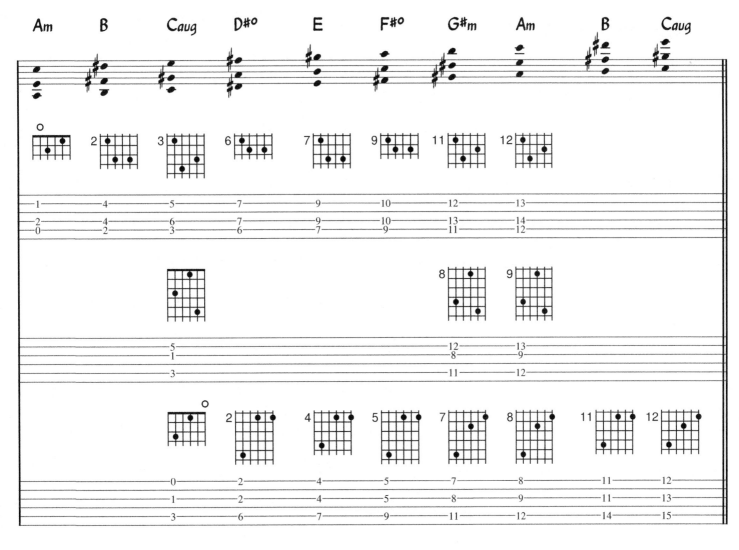

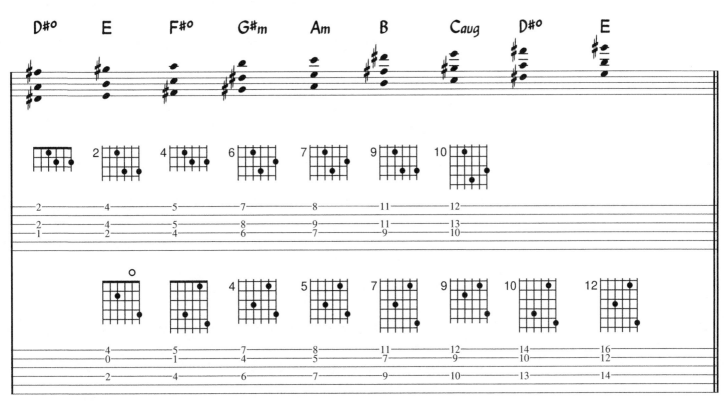

69

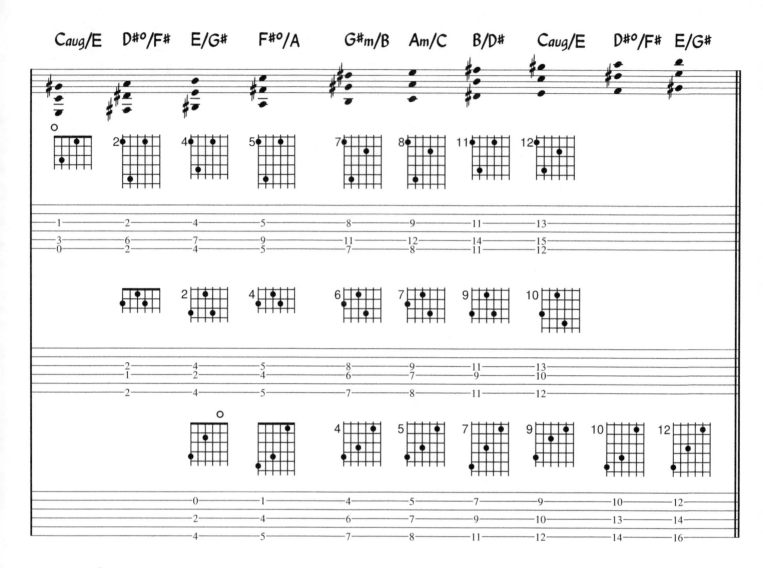

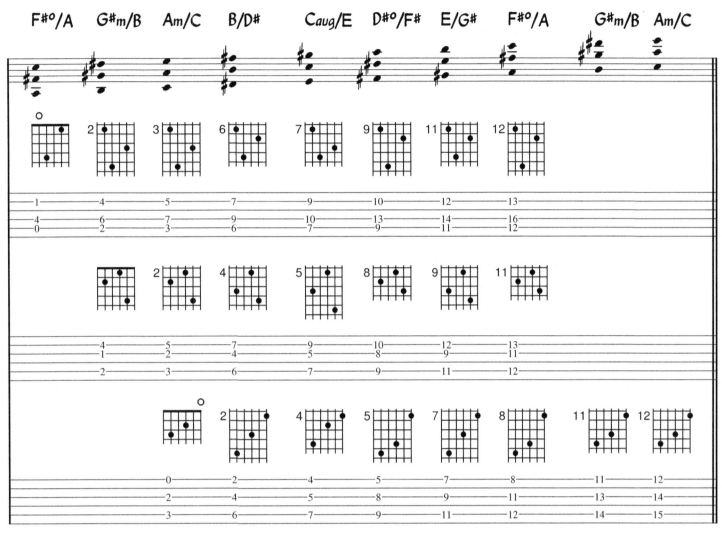

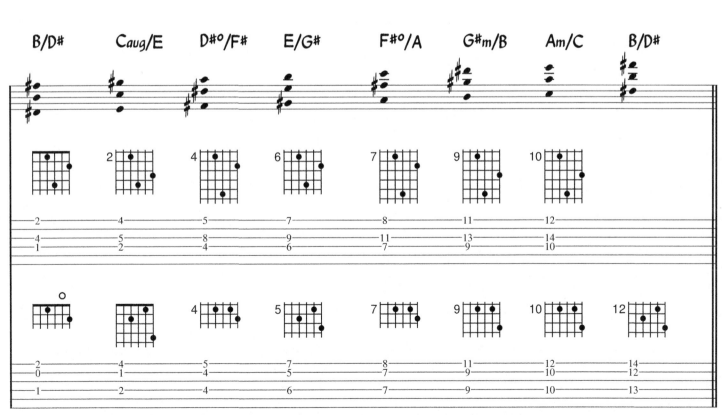

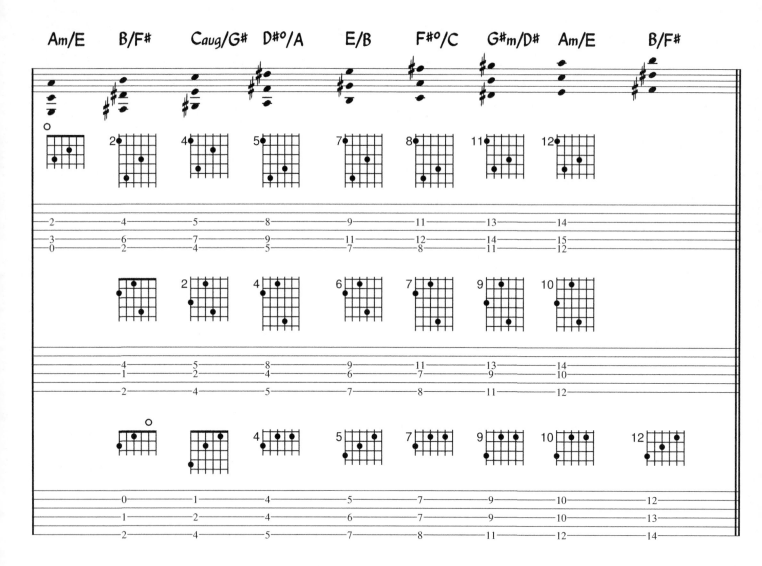

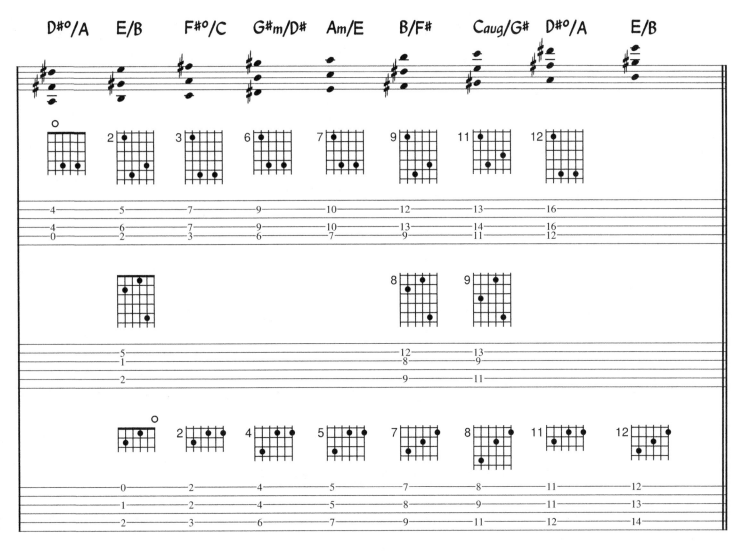

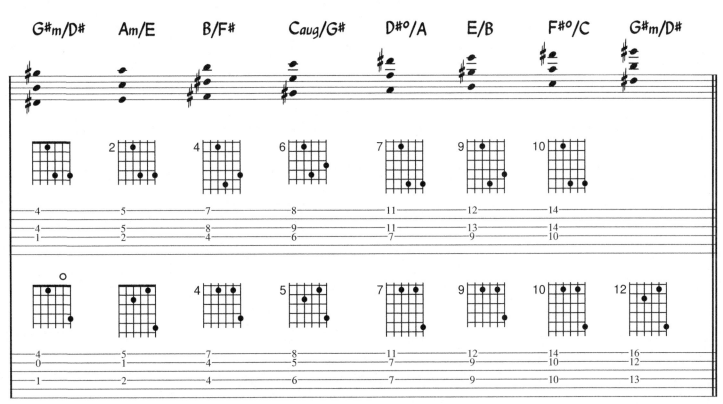

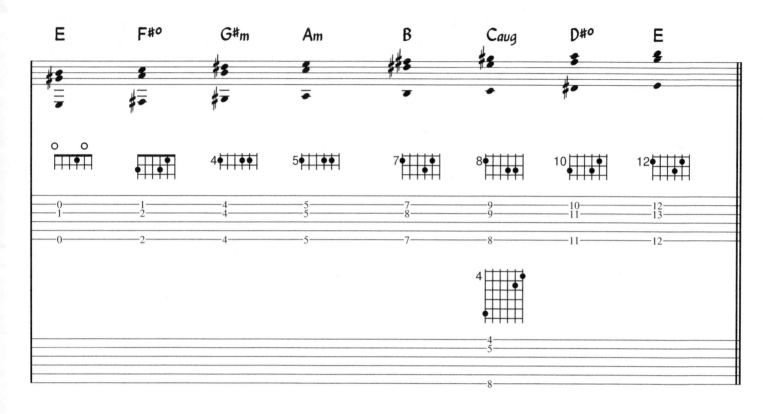

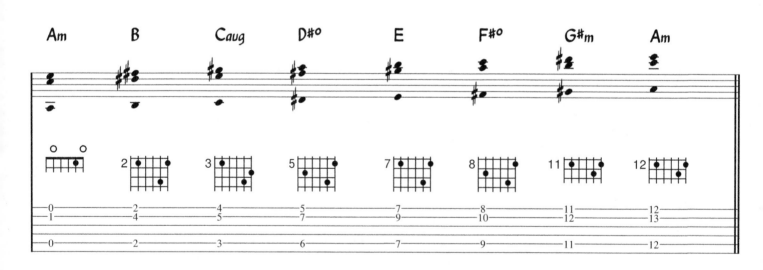

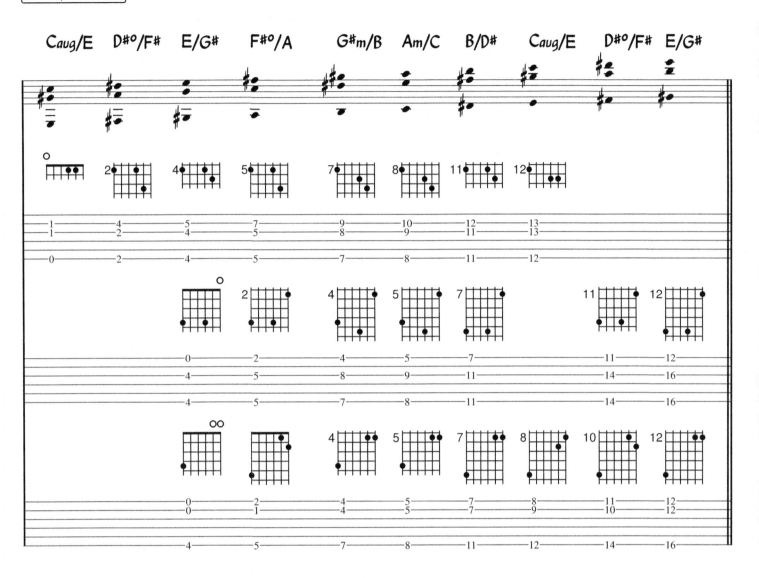

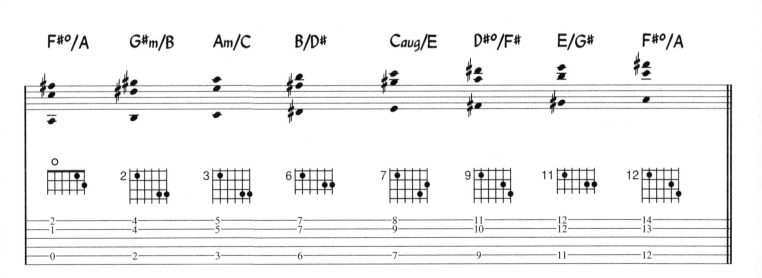

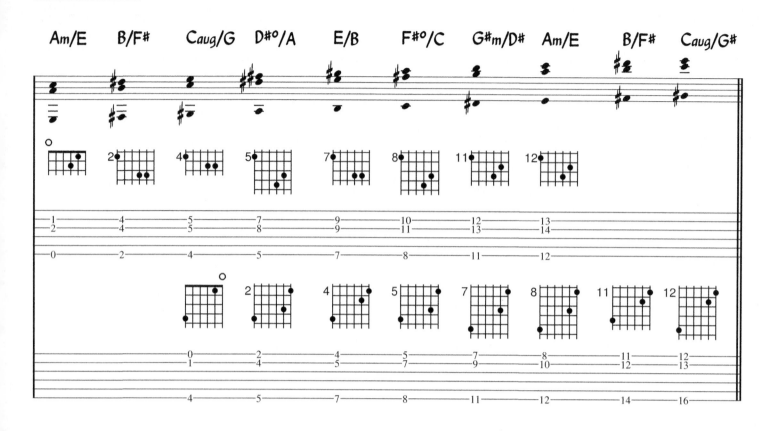

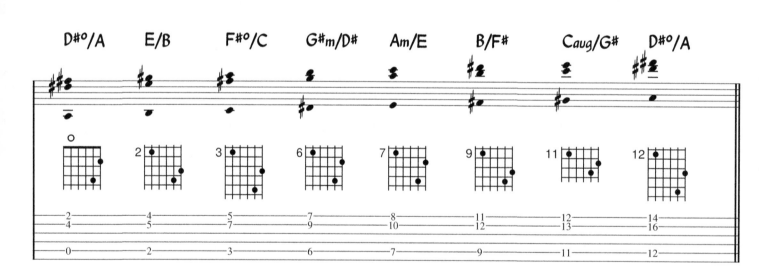

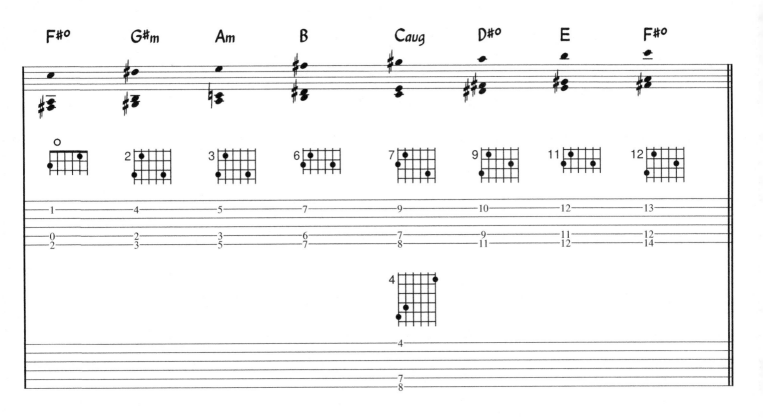

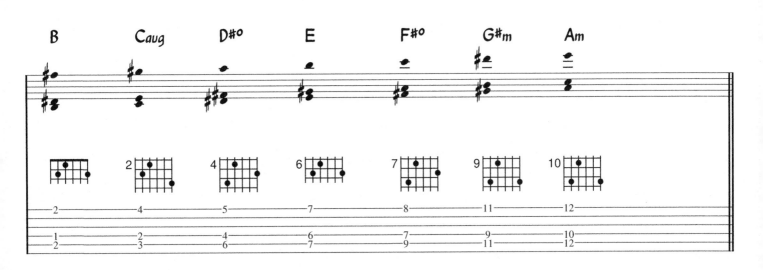

77

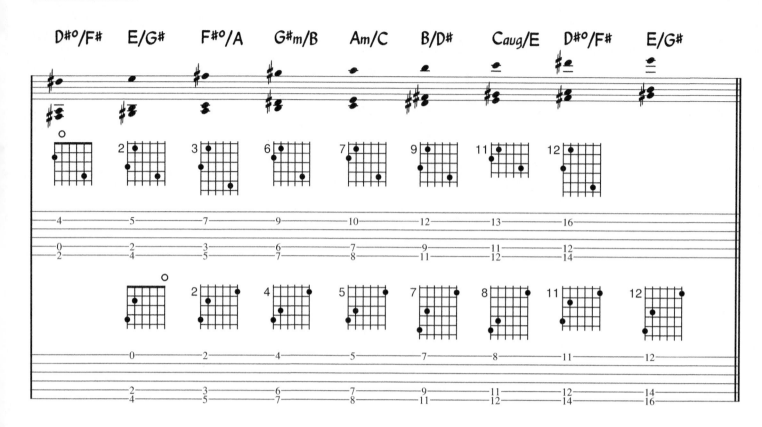

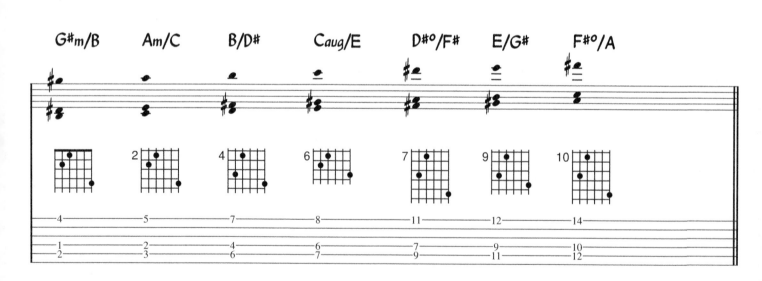

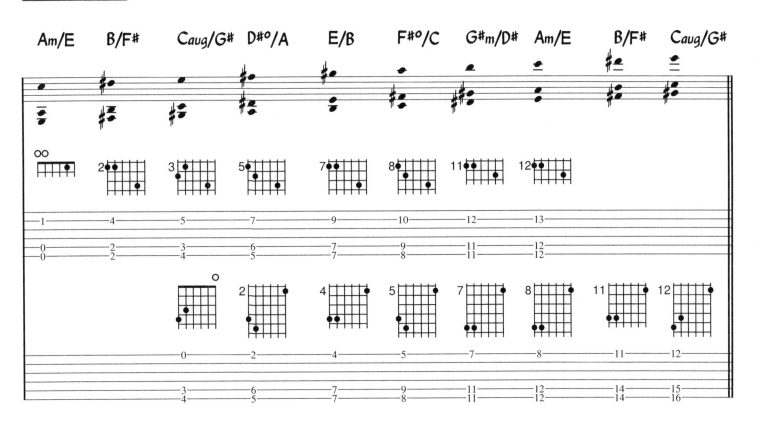

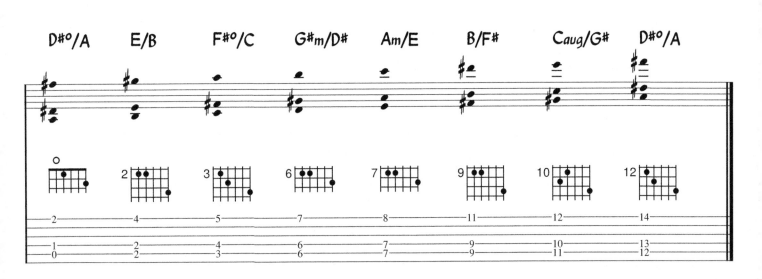

79

~ B harmonic major ~

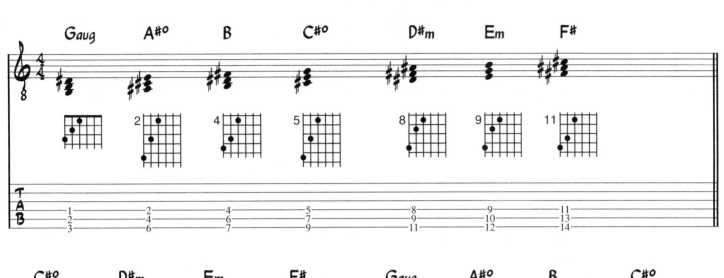

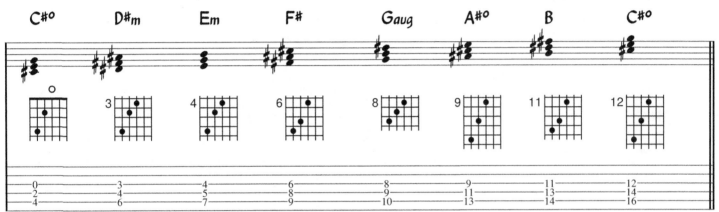

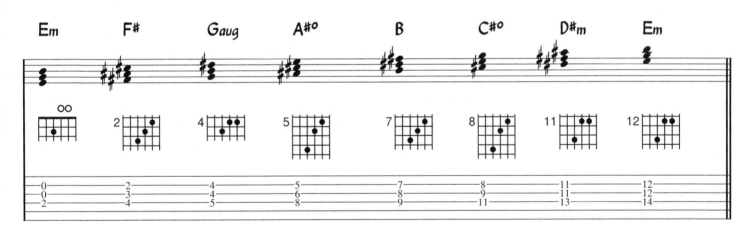

83

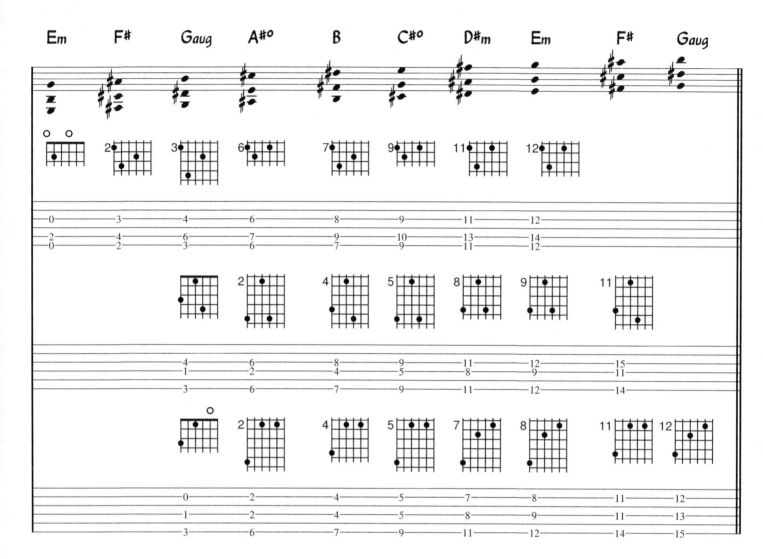

84

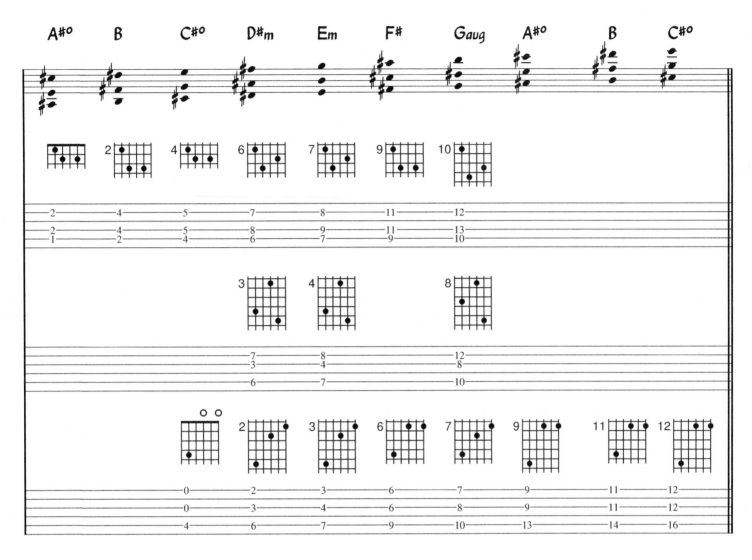

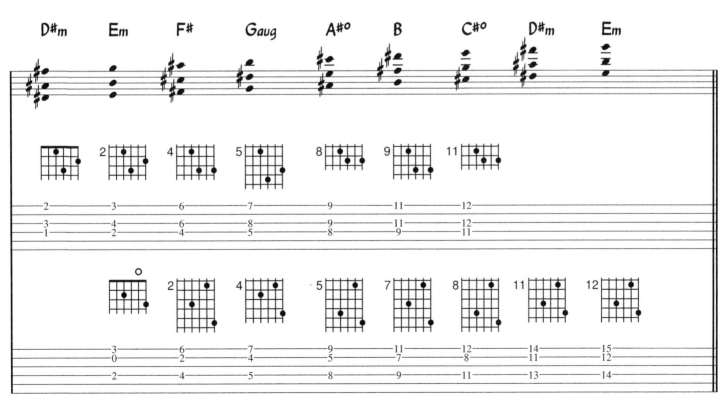

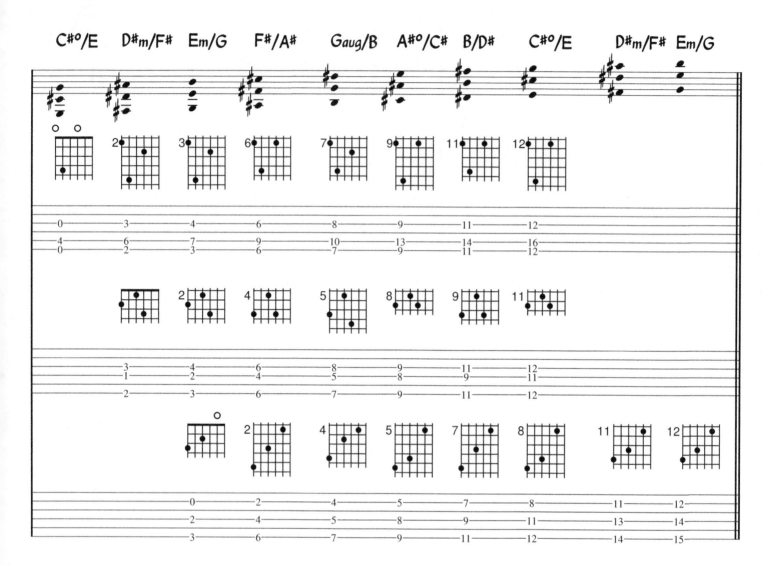

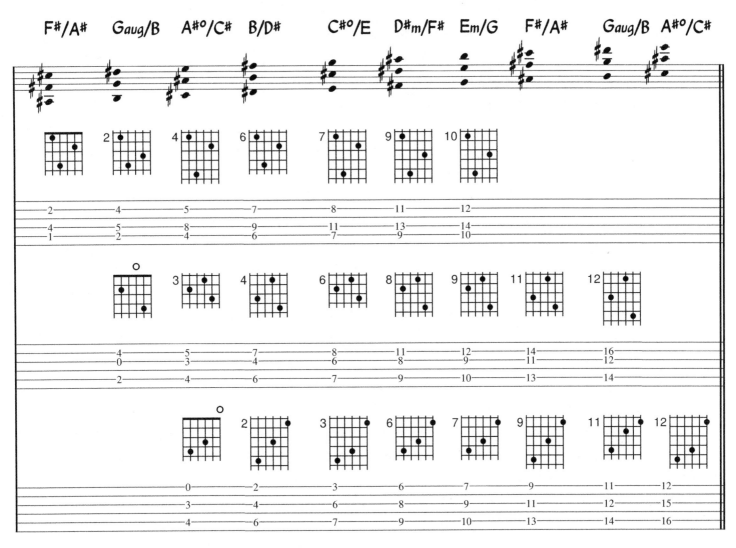

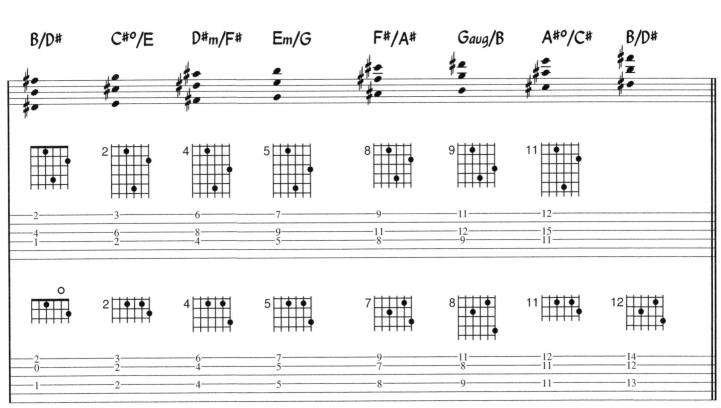

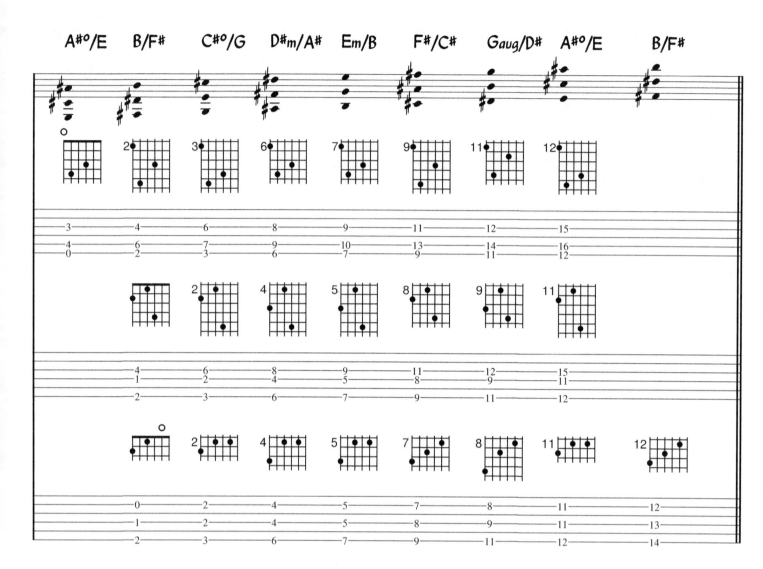

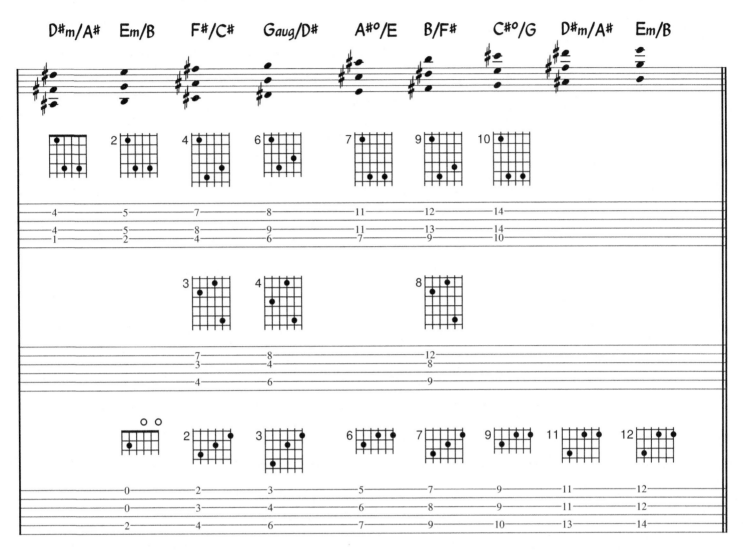

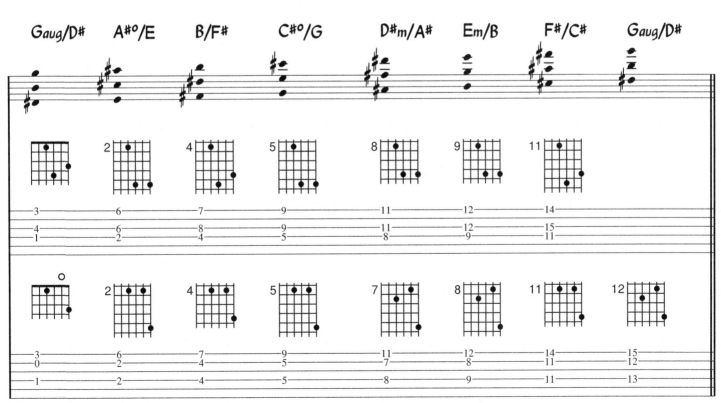

89

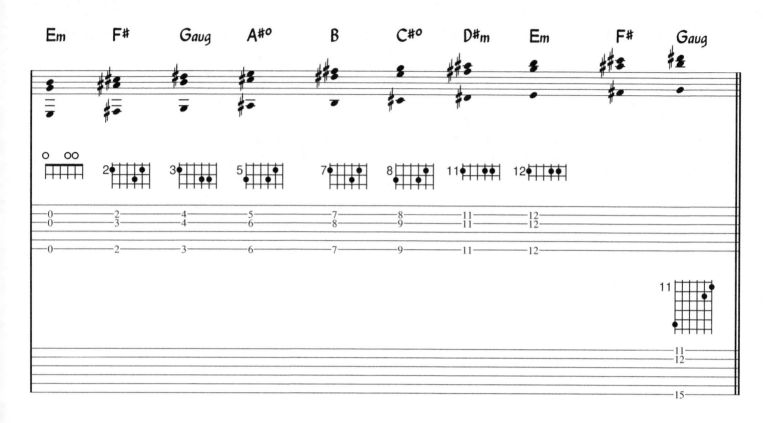

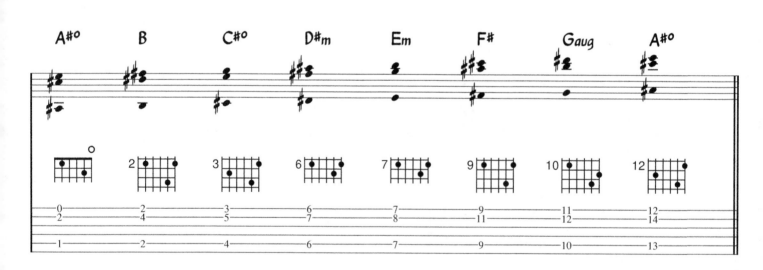

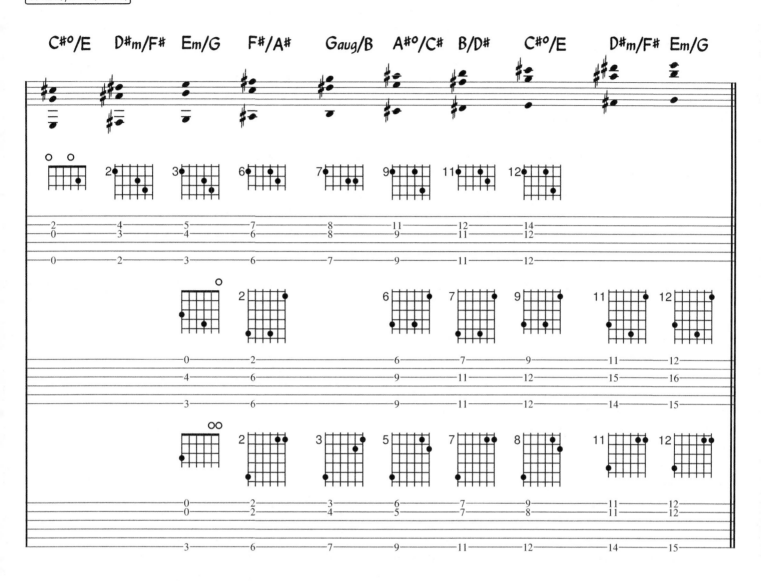

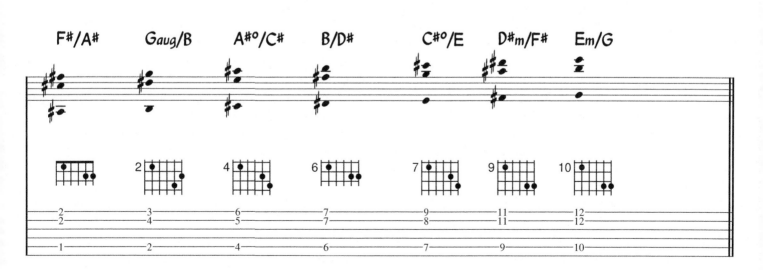

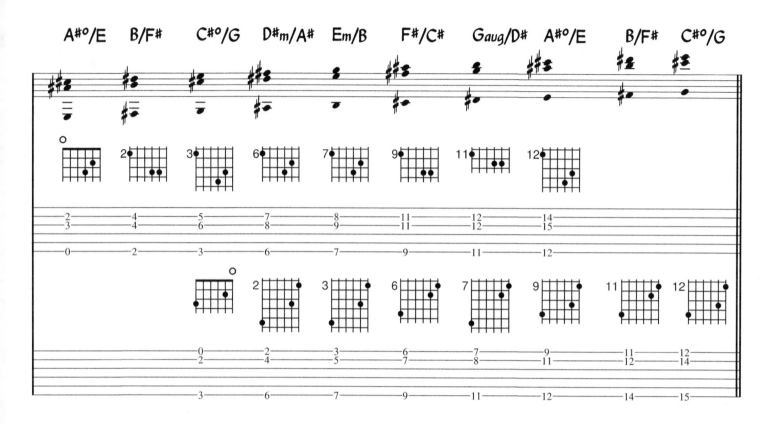

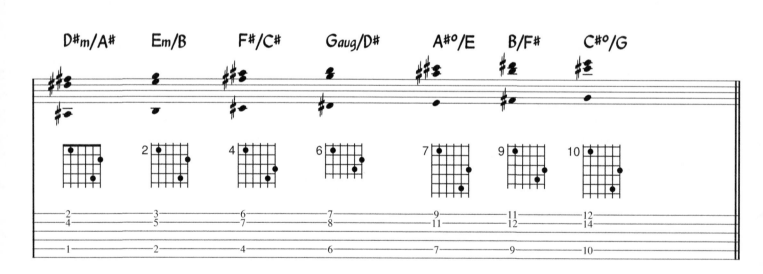

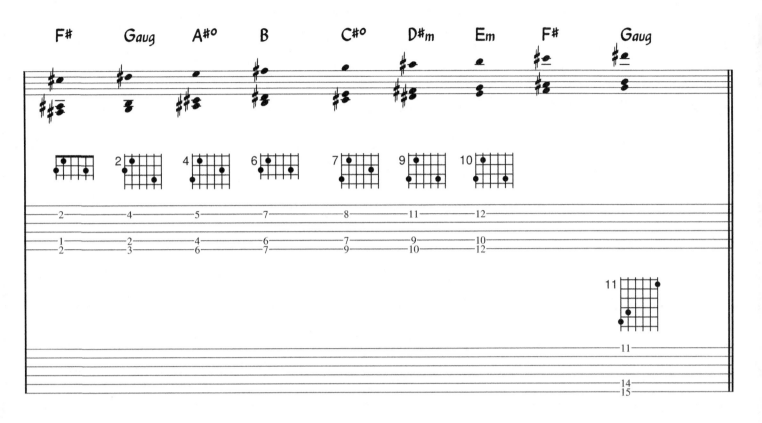

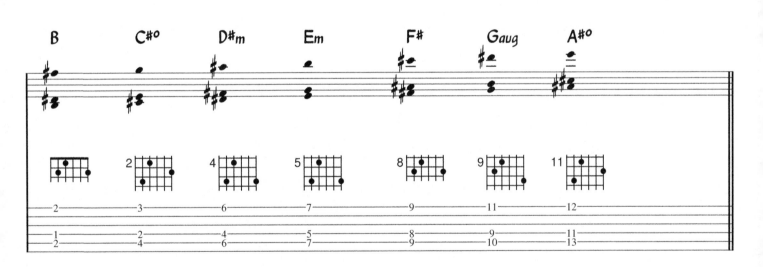

93

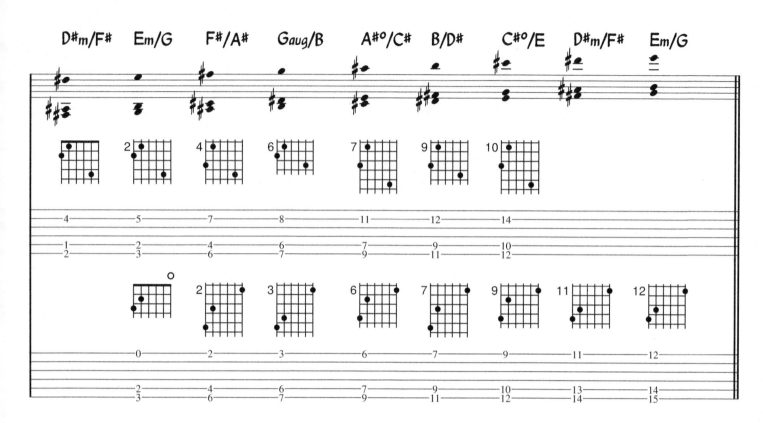

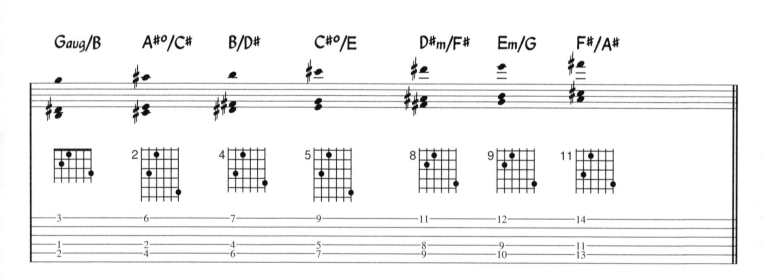

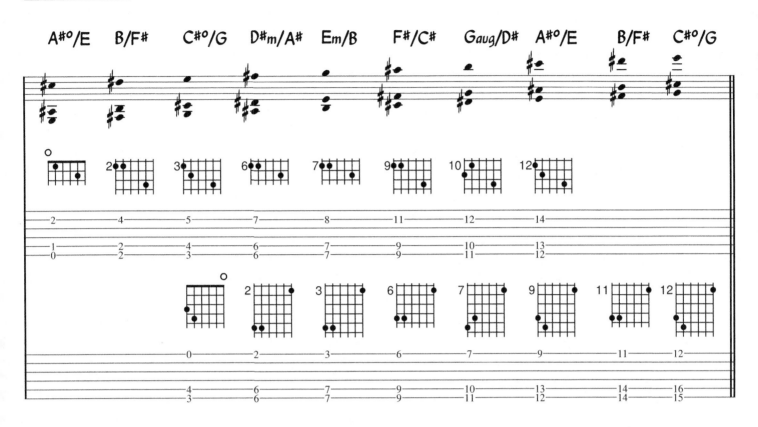

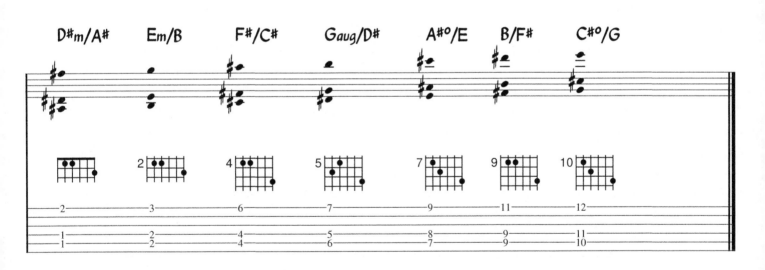

95

~ G♭ harmonic major ~

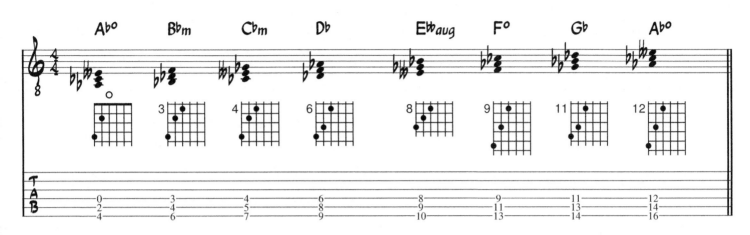

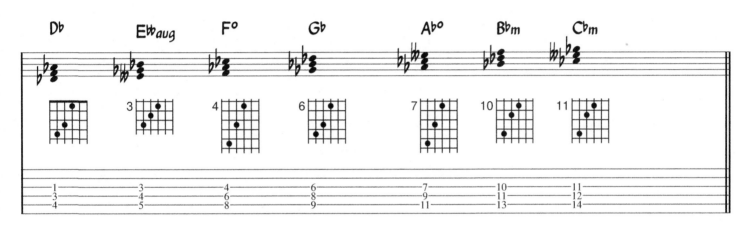

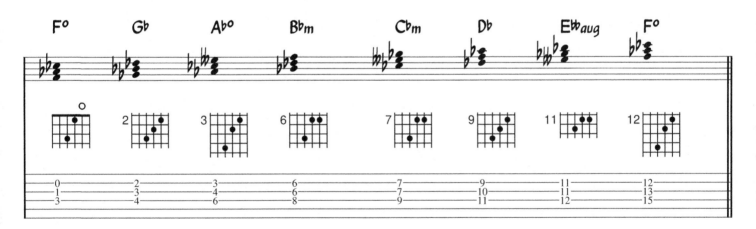

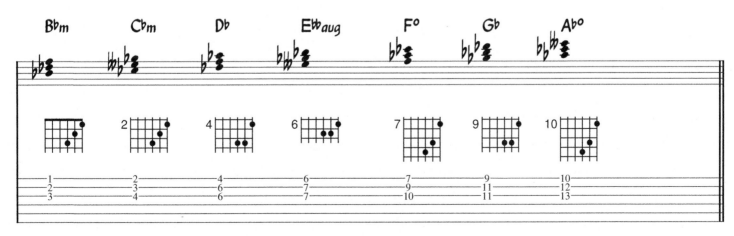

98

99

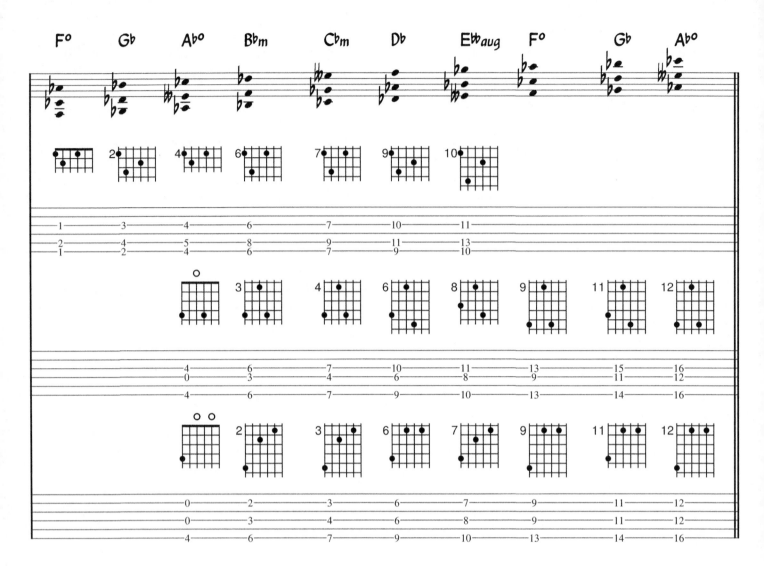

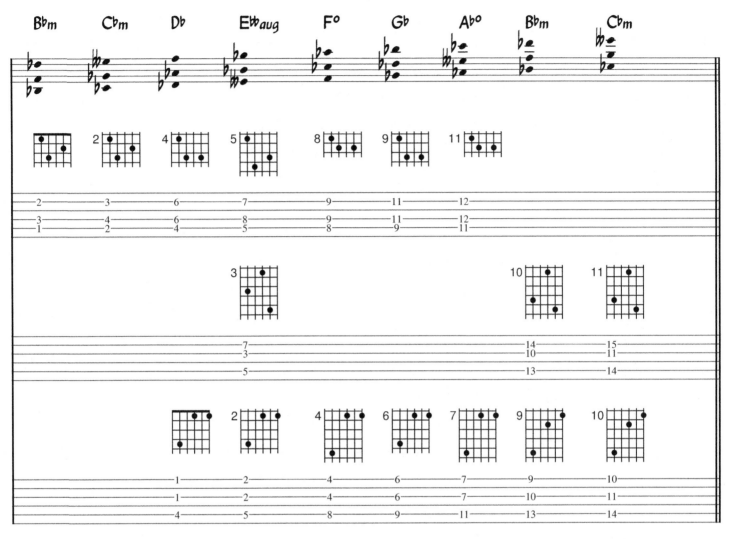

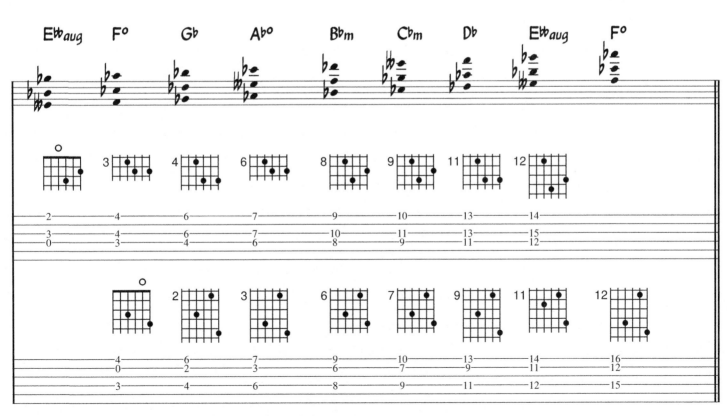

101

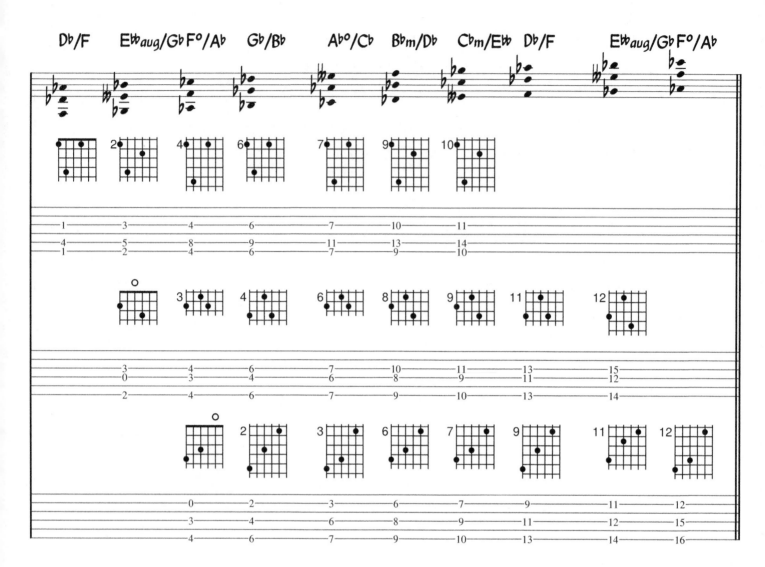

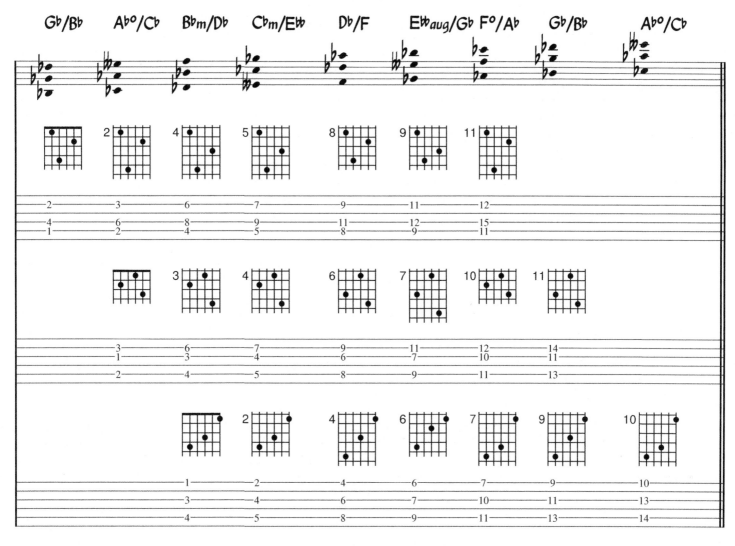

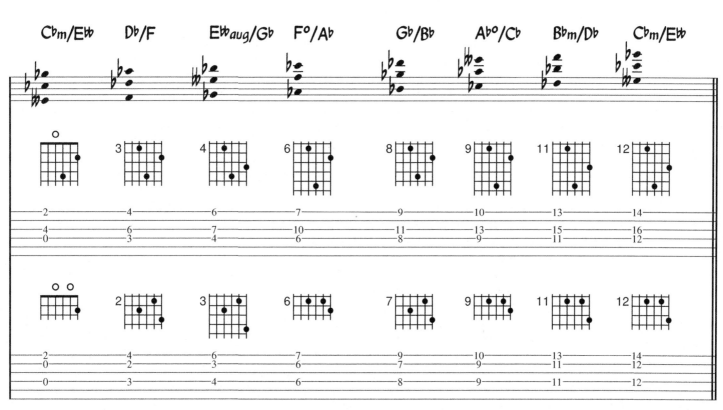

103

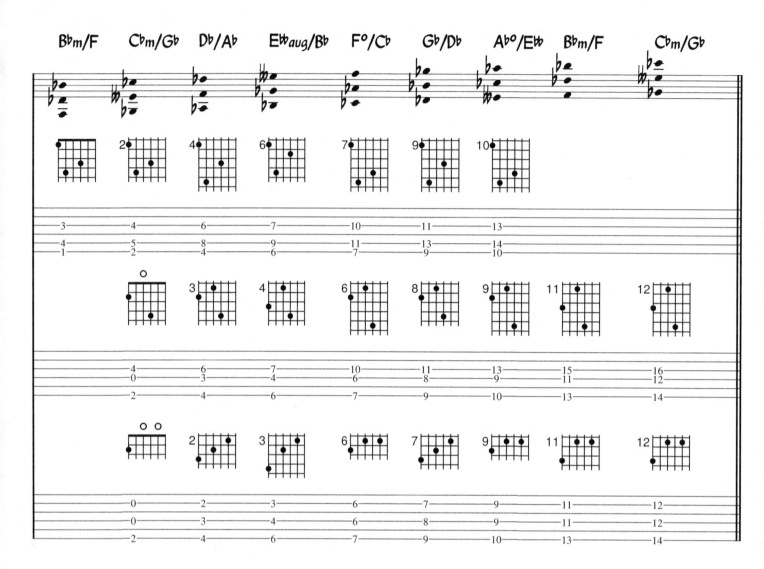

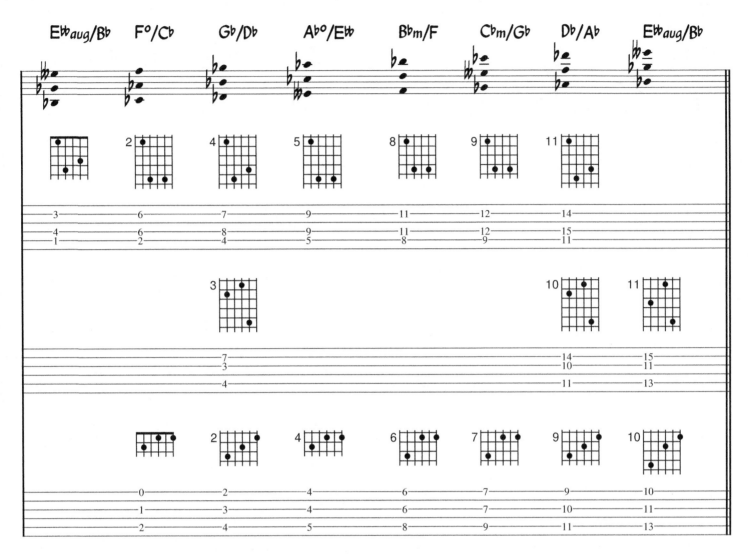

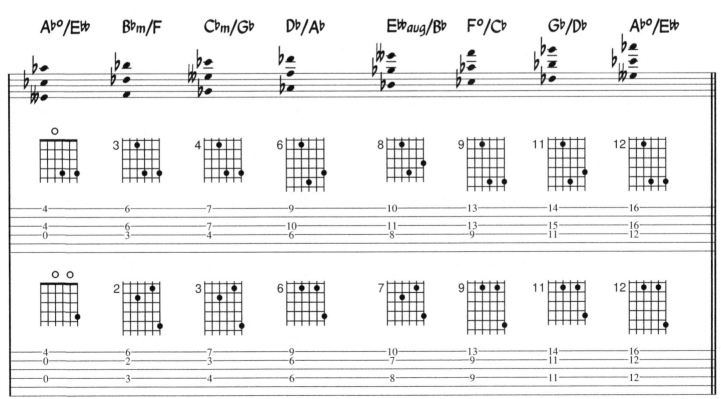

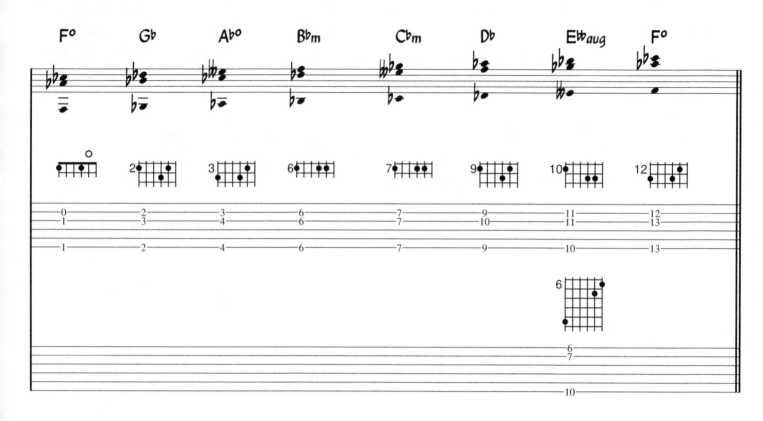

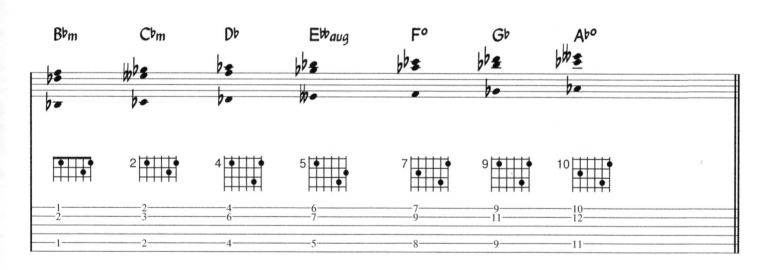

106

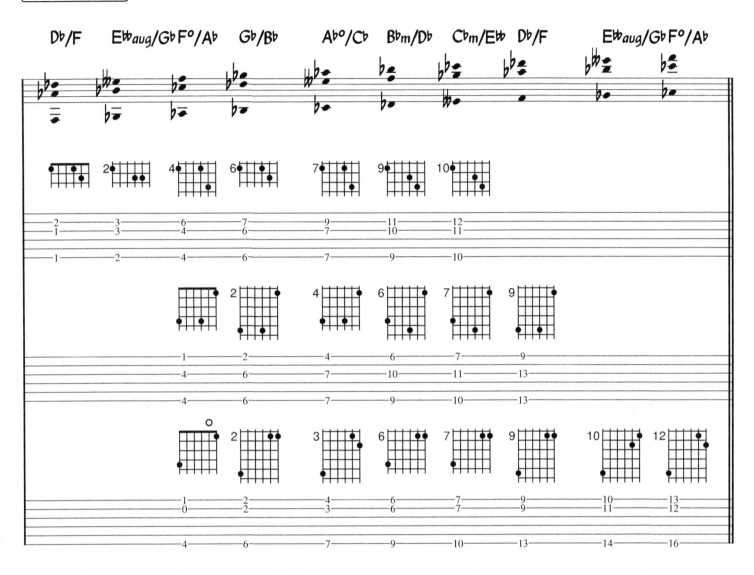

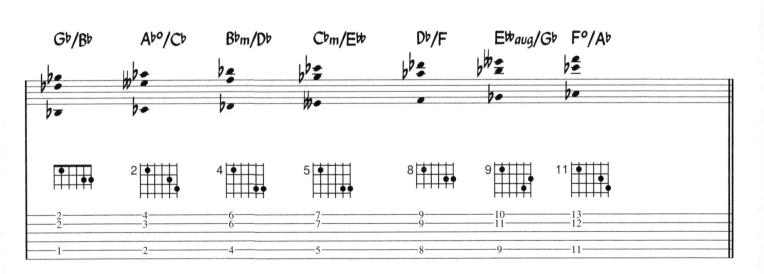

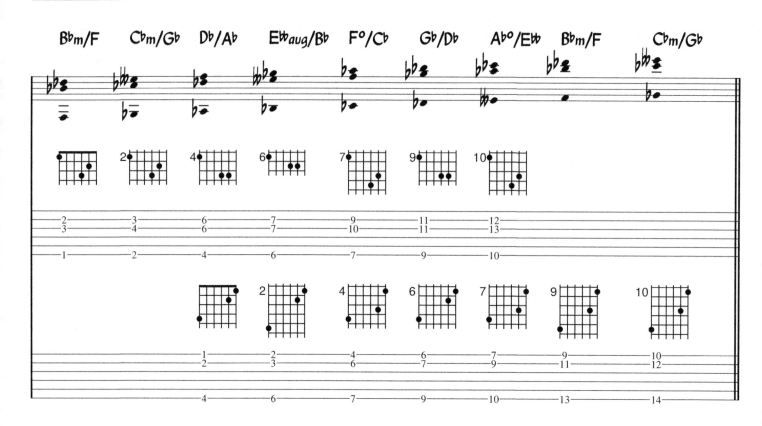

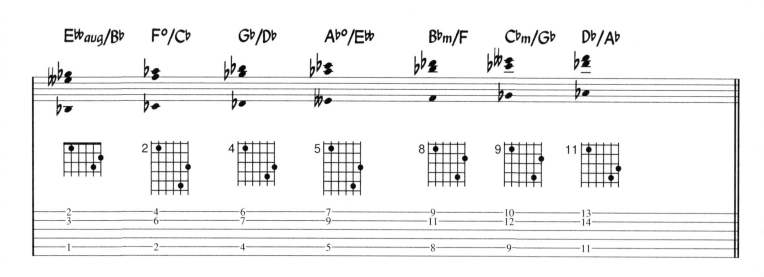

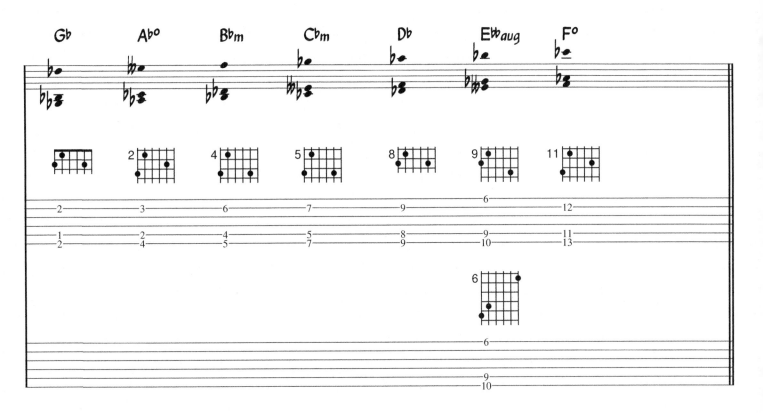

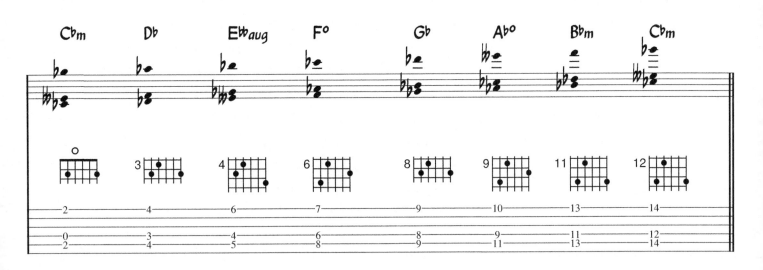

109

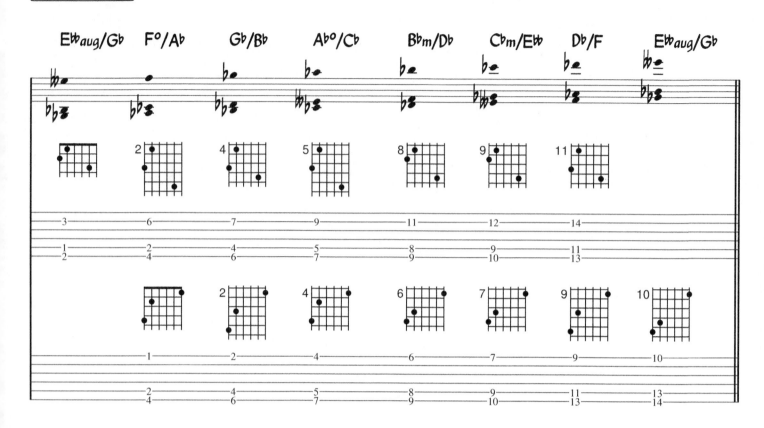

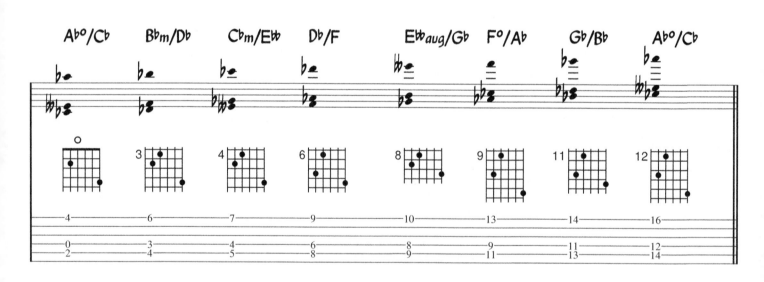

110

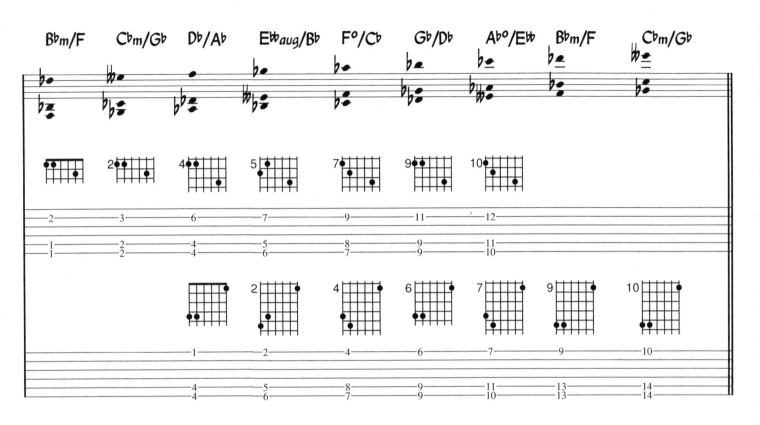

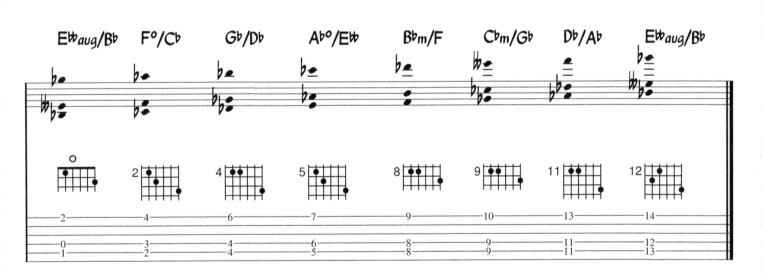

111

~ D♭ harmonic major ~

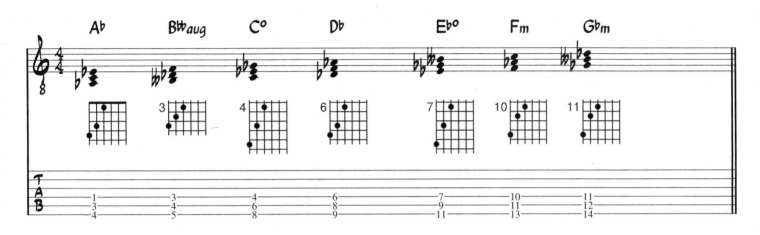

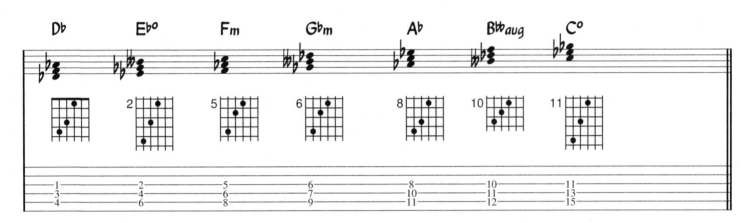

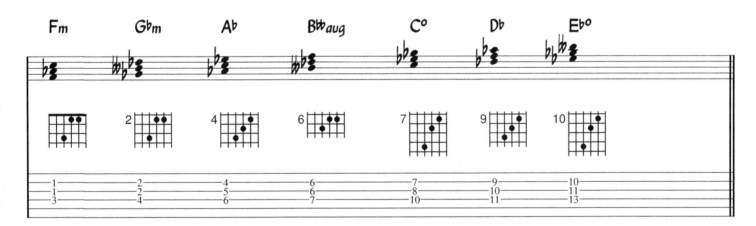

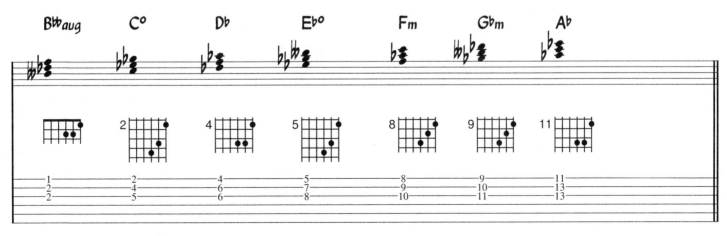

114

115

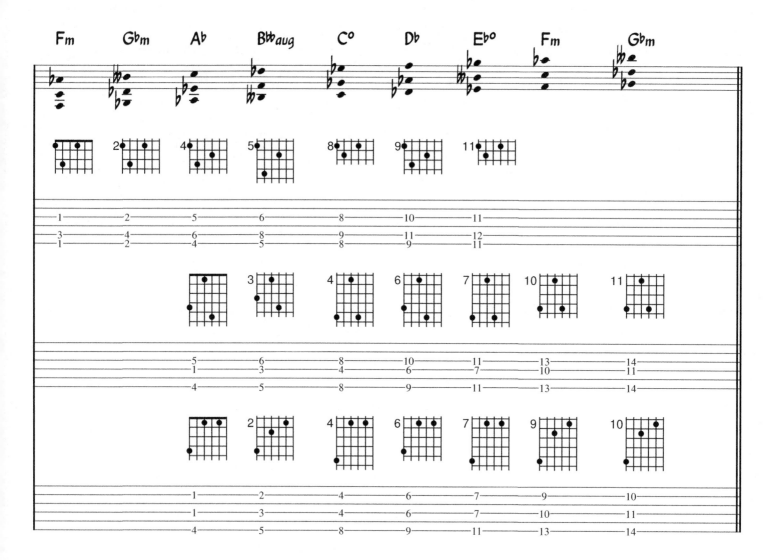

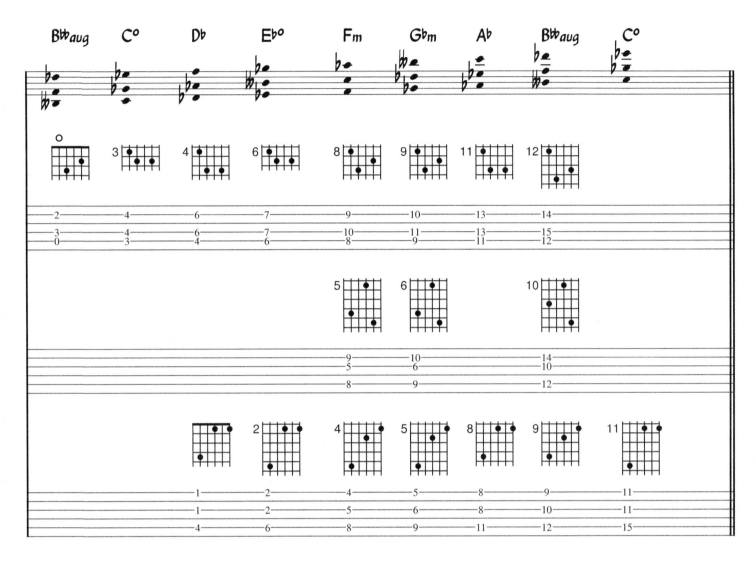

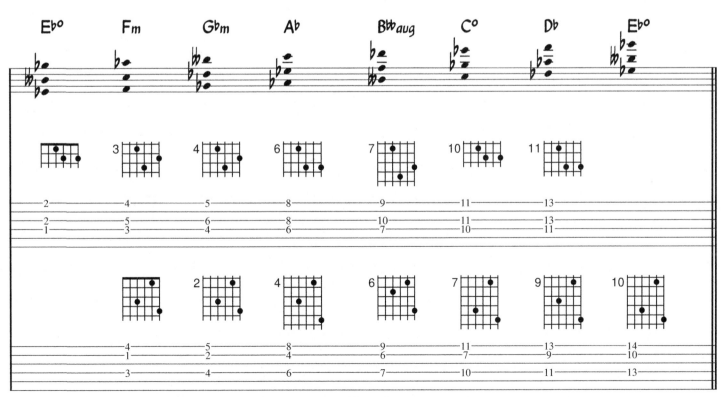

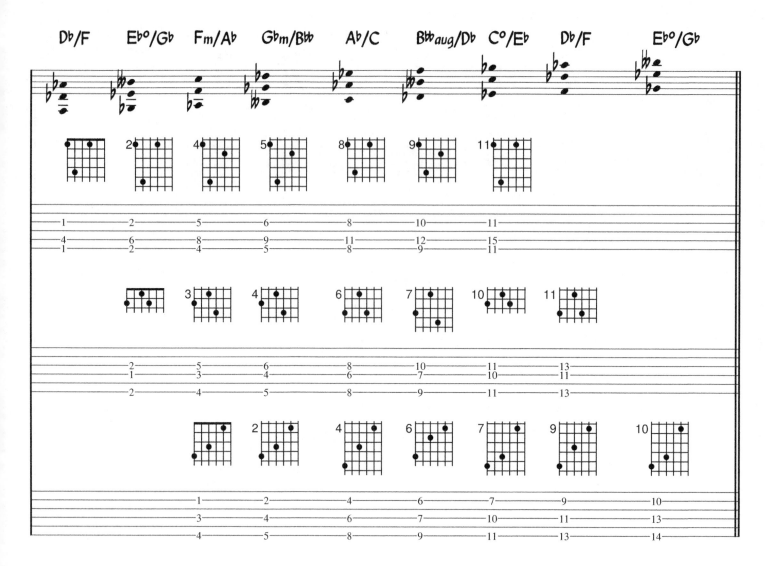

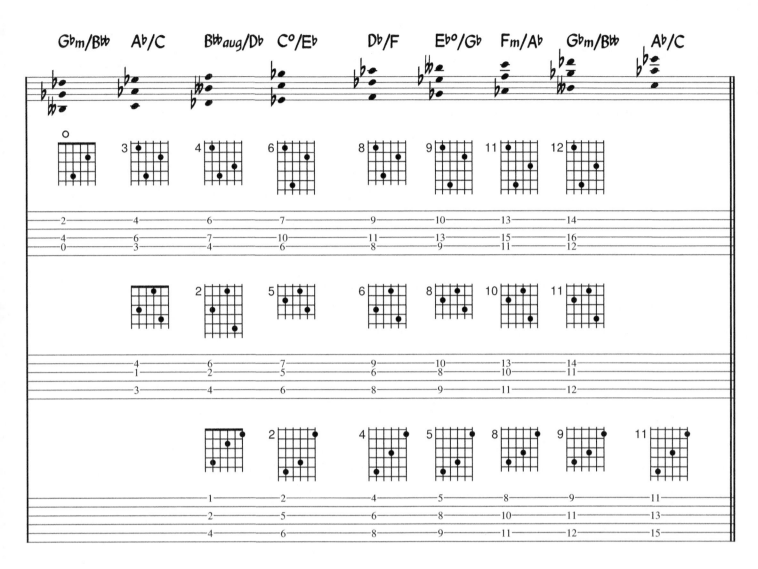

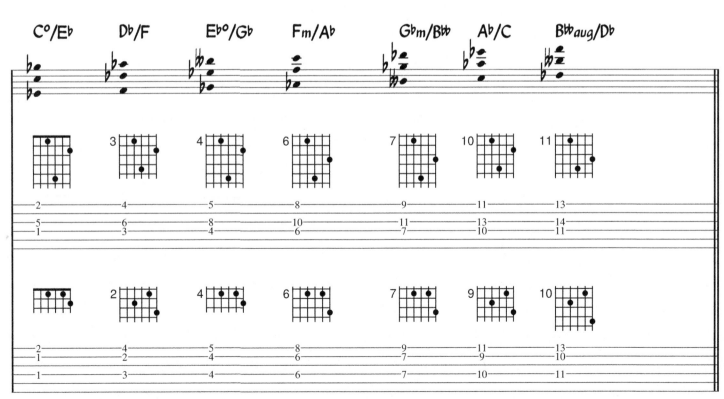

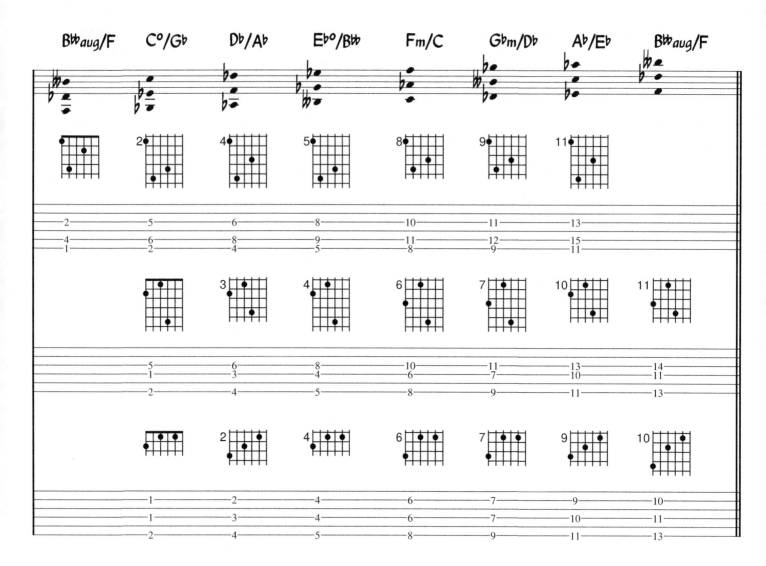

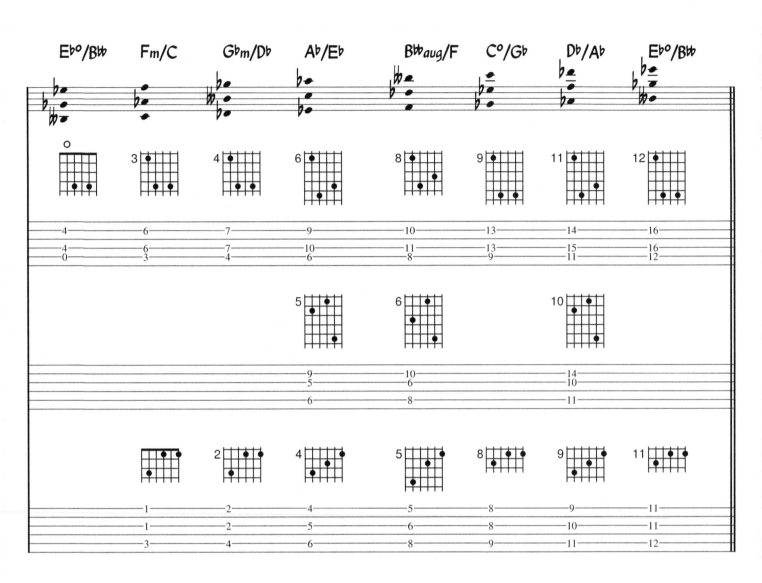

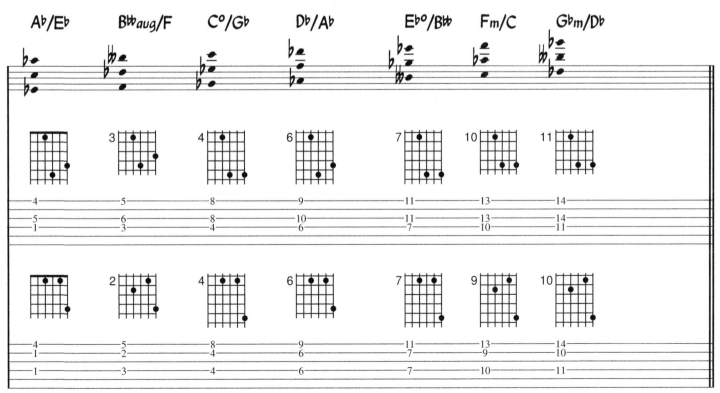

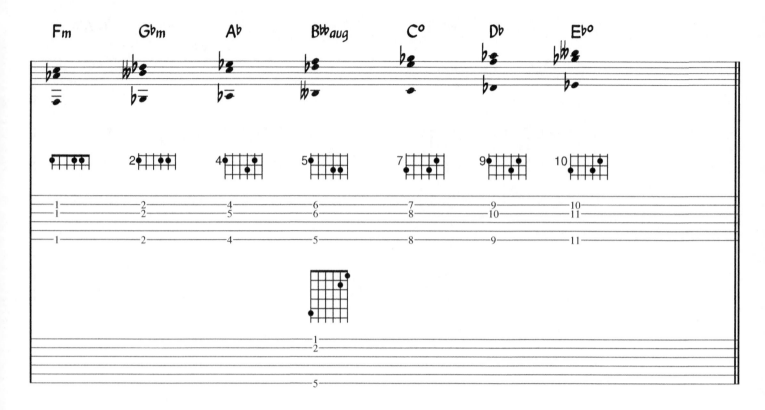

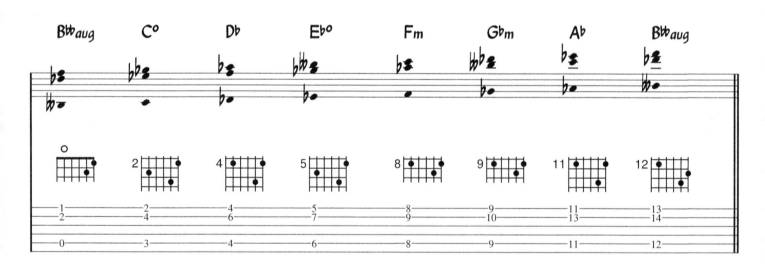

122

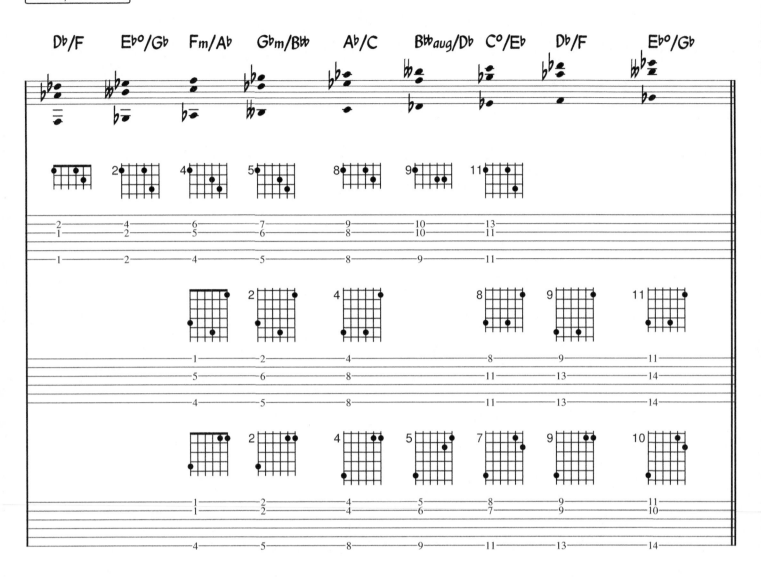

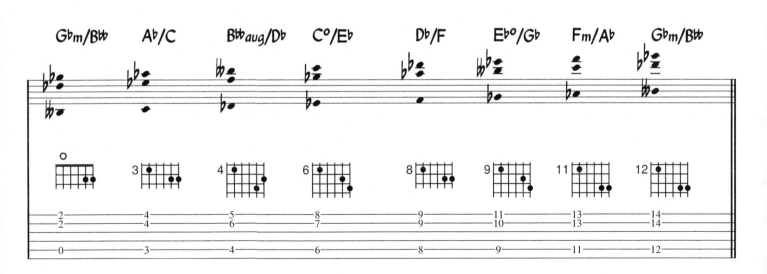

123

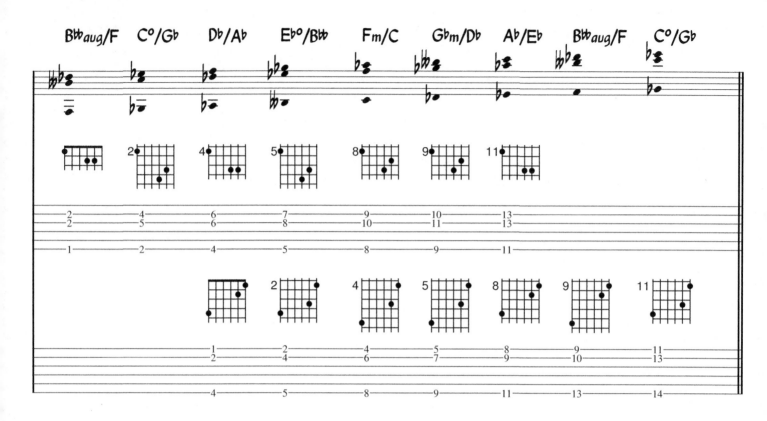

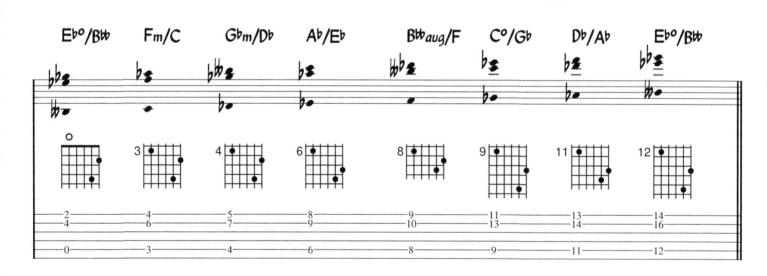

124

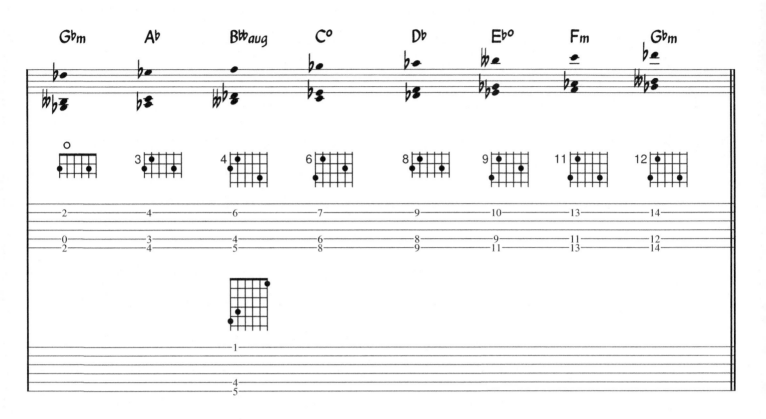

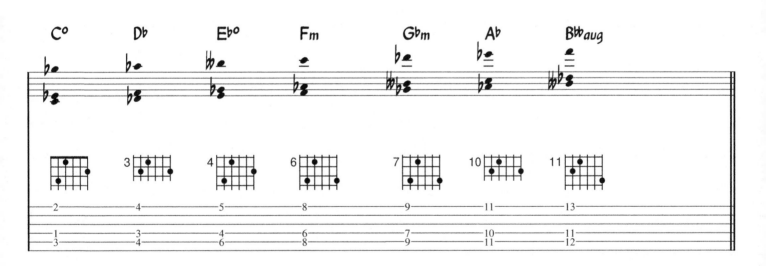

125

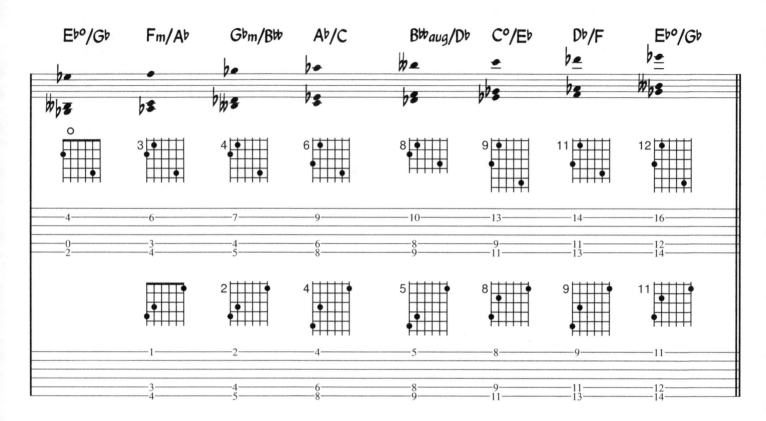

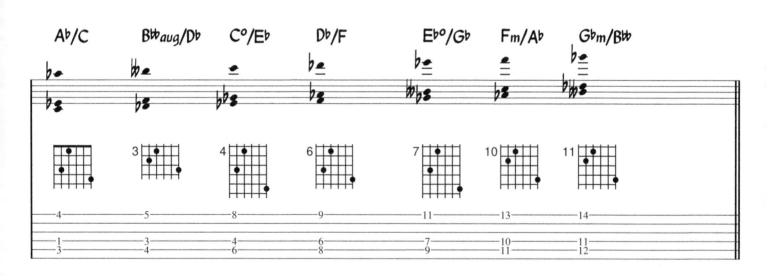

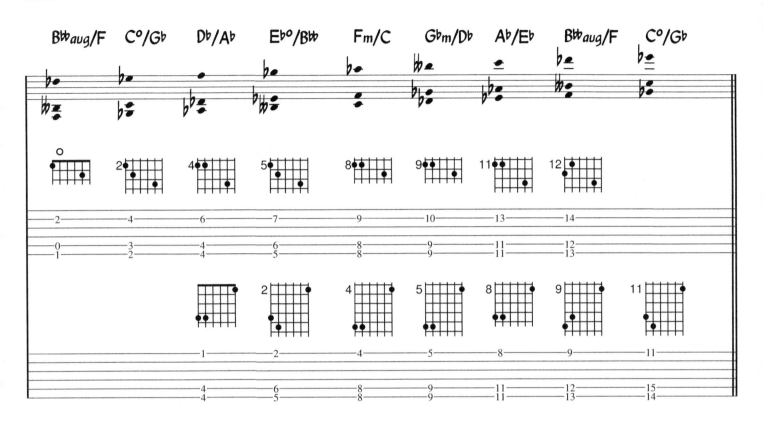

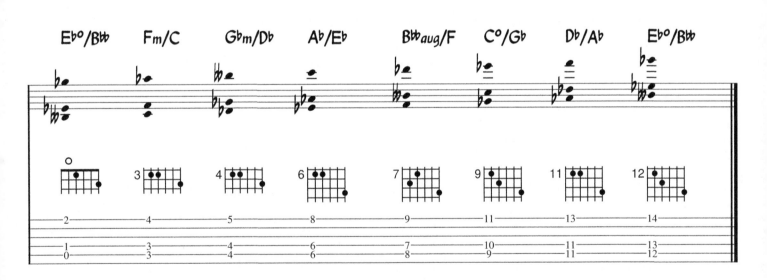

127

~ A♭ harmonic major ~

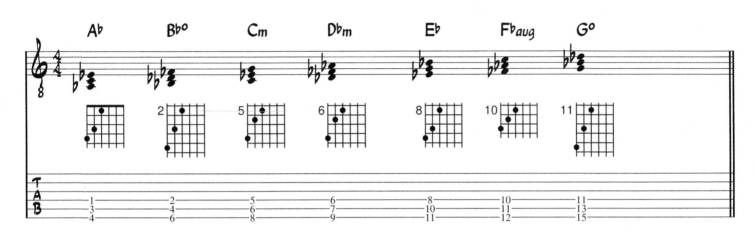

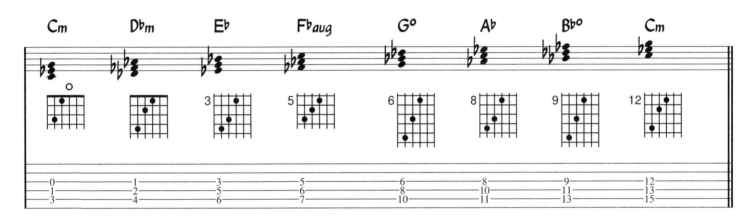

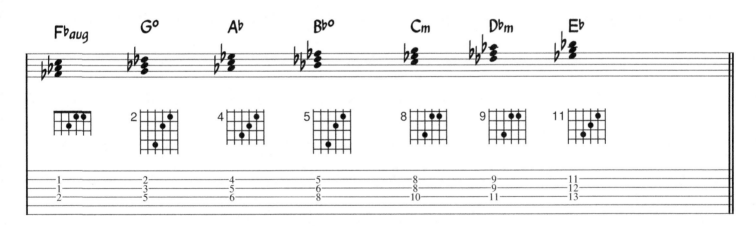

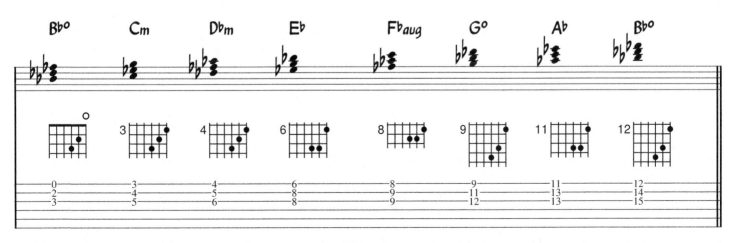

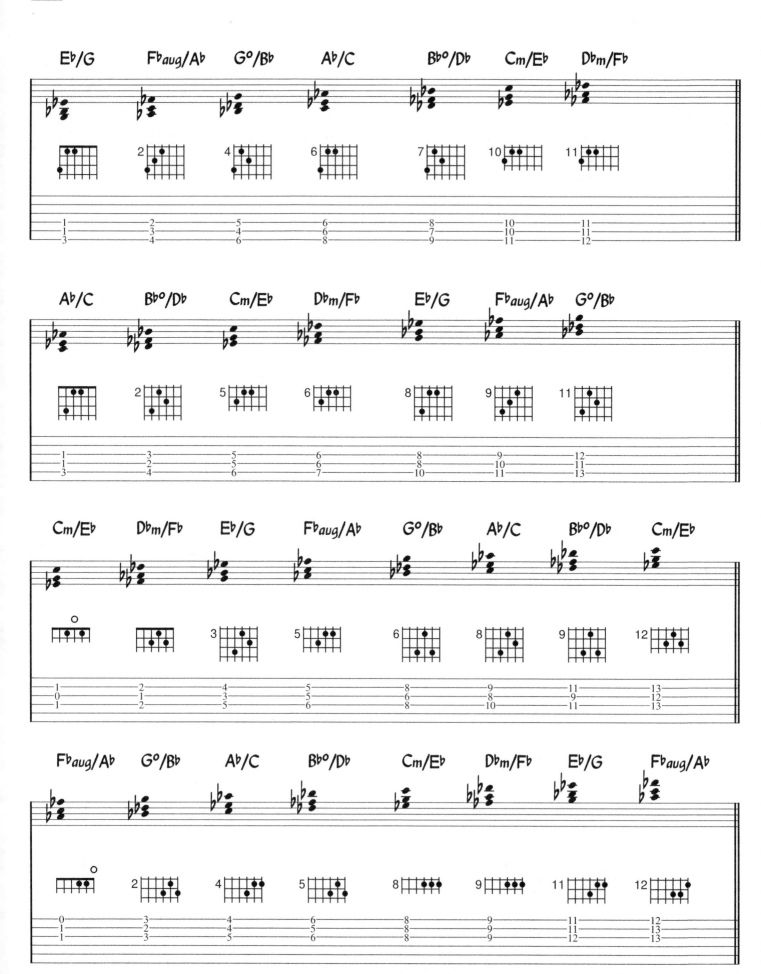

130

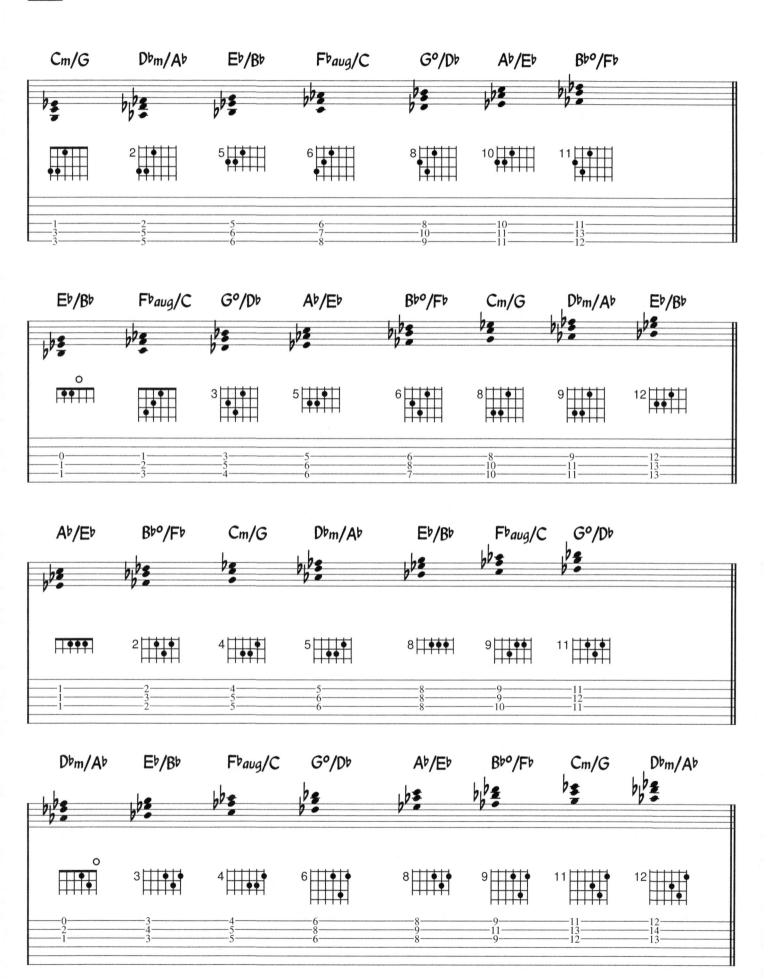

131

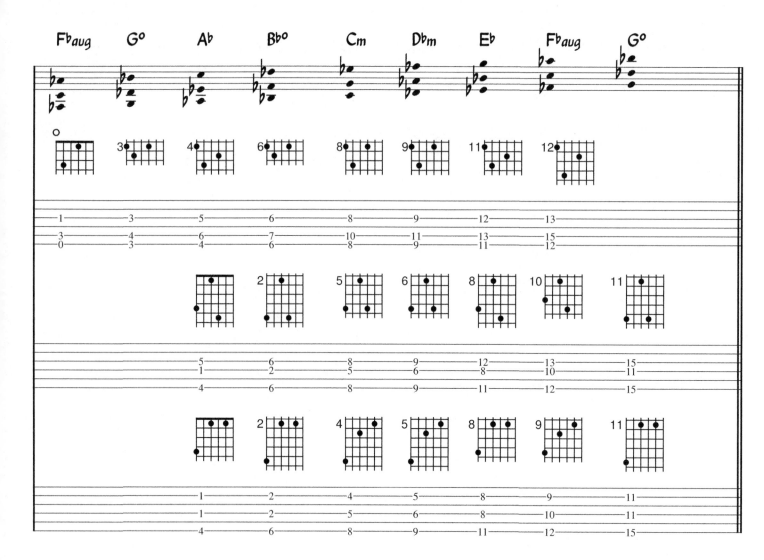

132

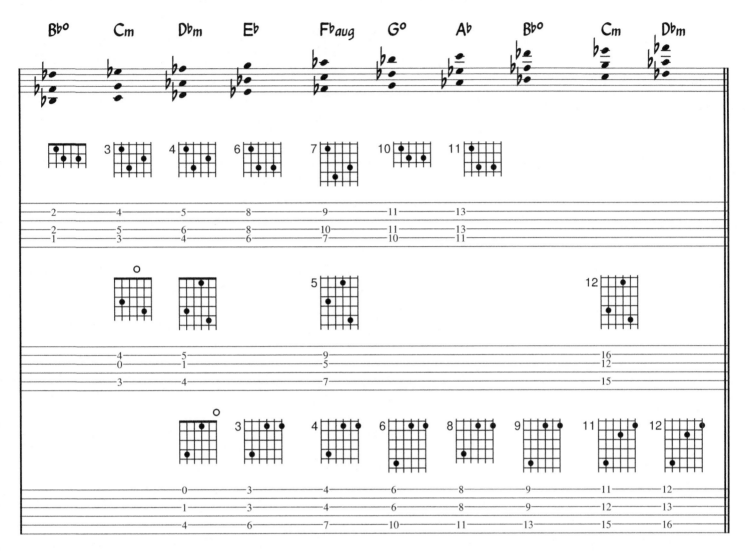

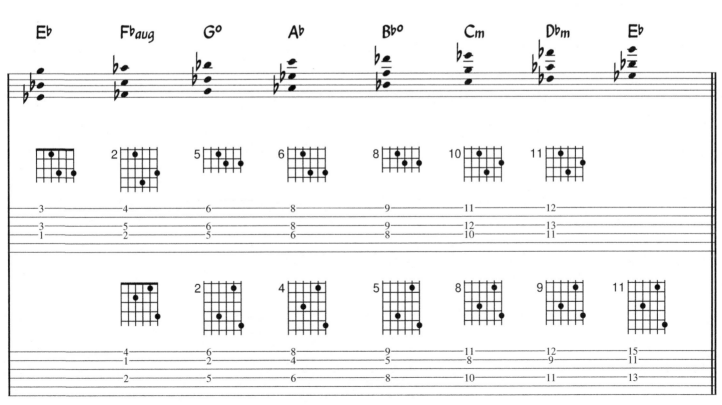

133

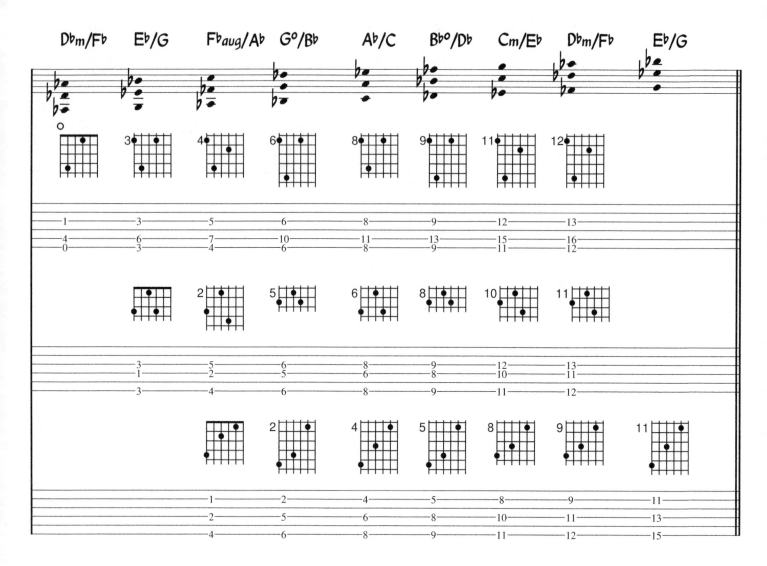

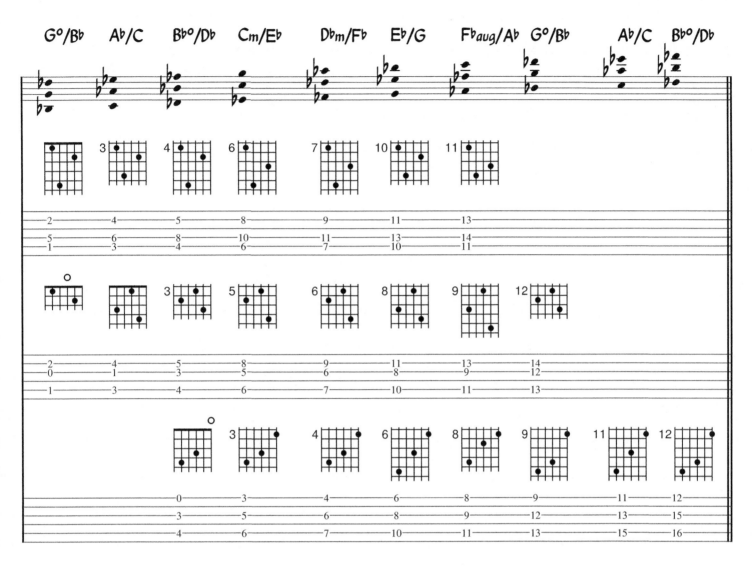

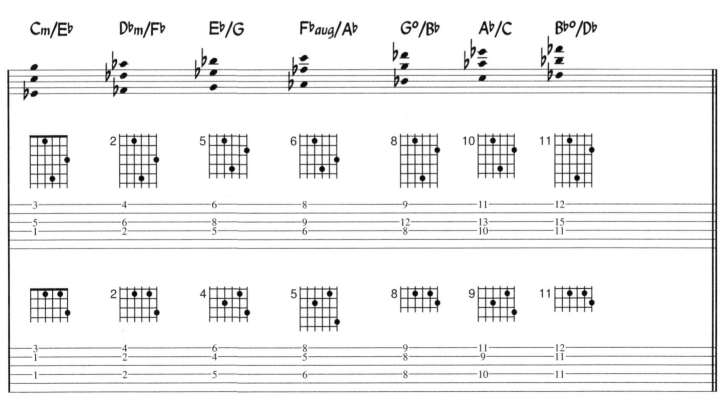

135

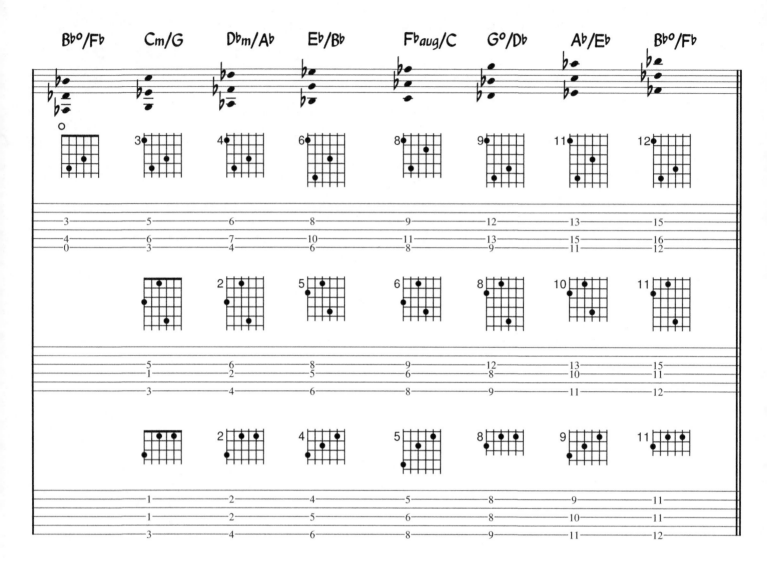

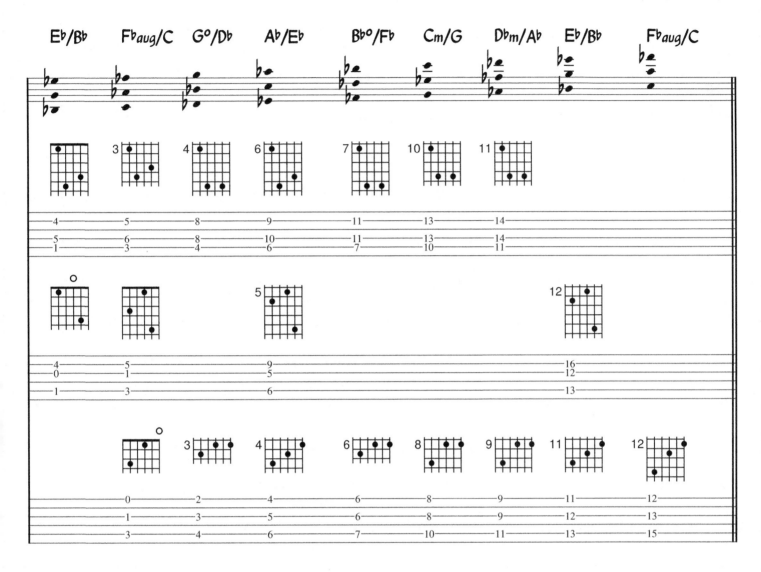

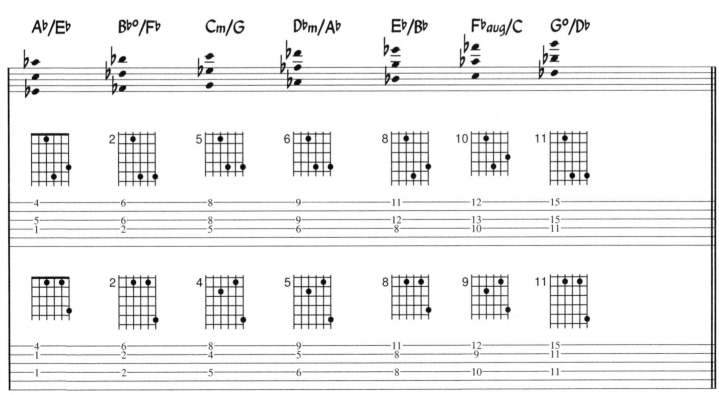

137

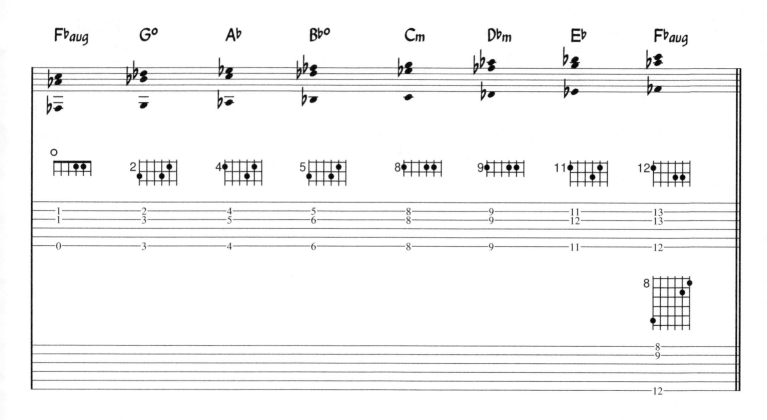

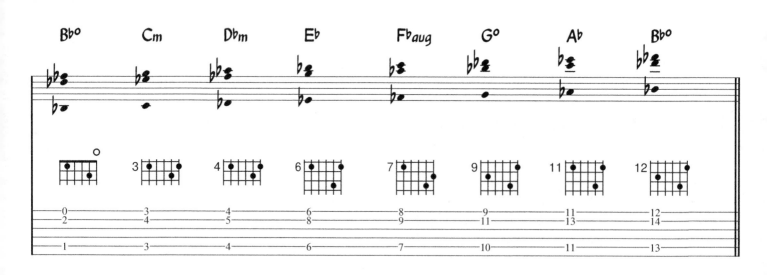

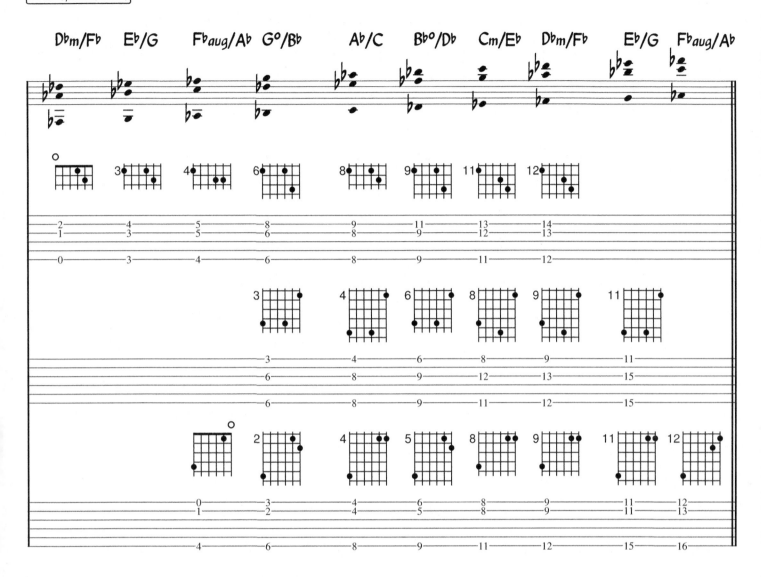

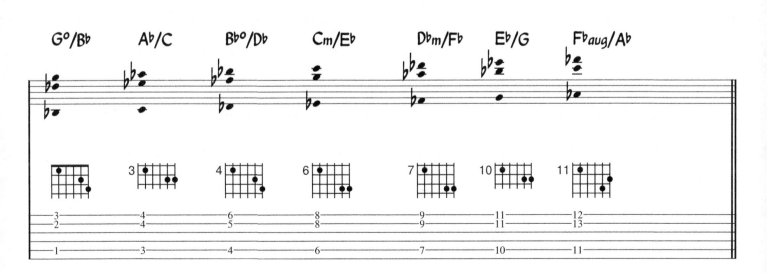

139

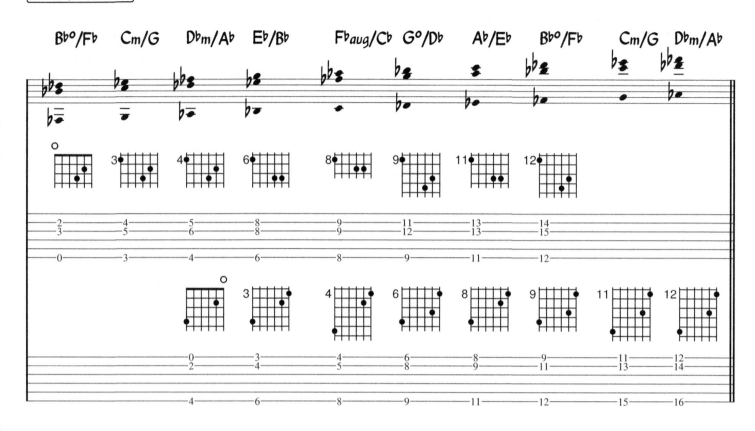

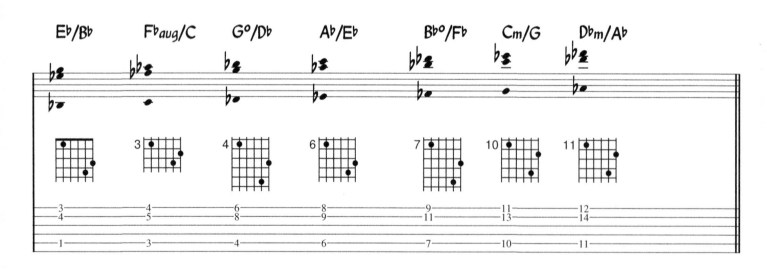

140

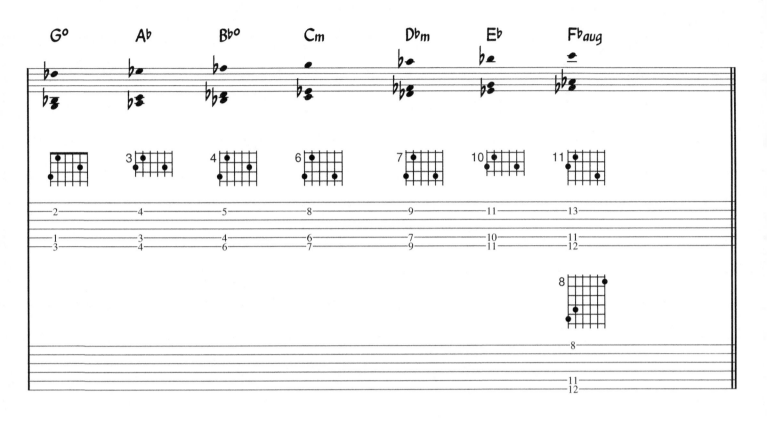

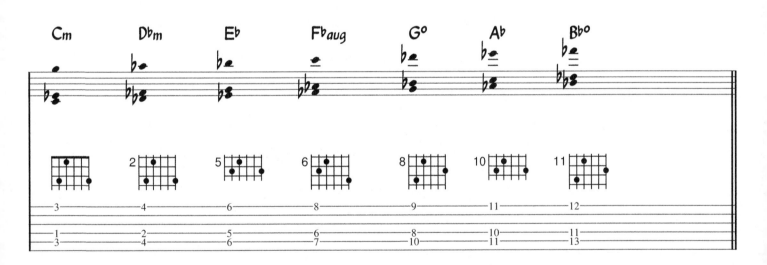

141

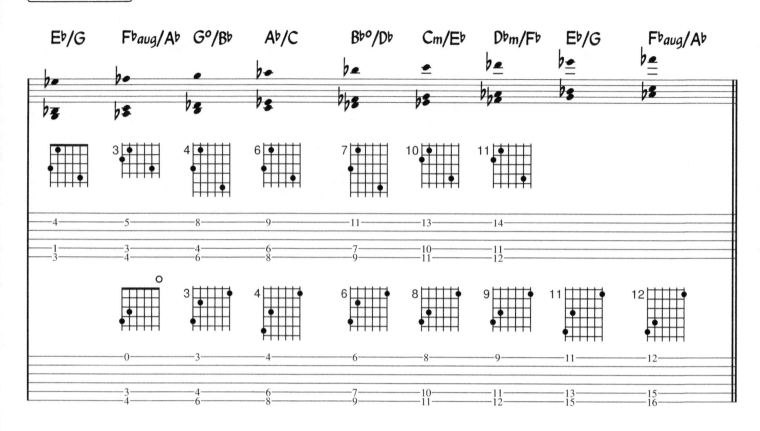

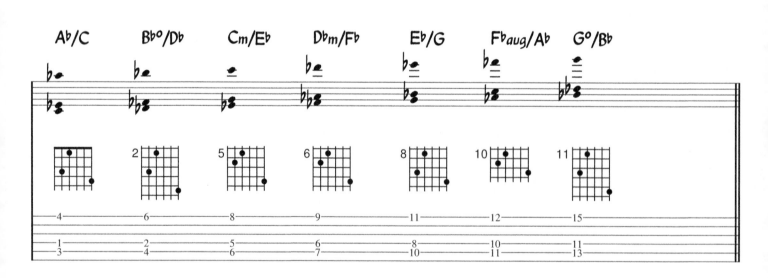

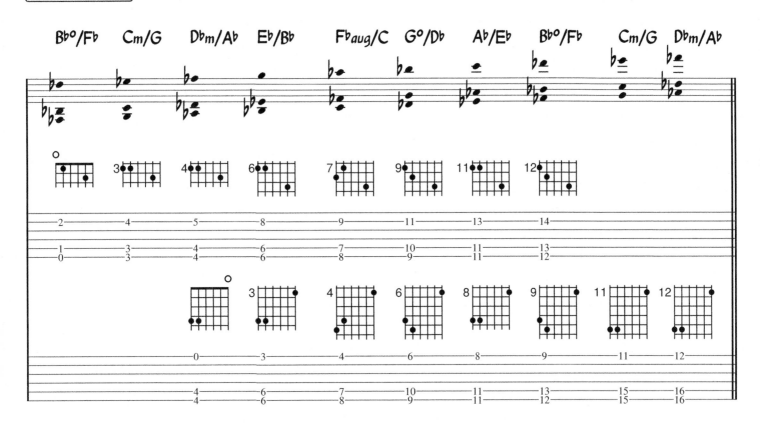

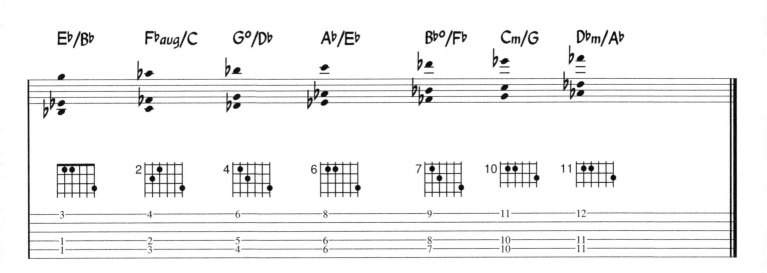

143

~ E♭ harmonic major ~

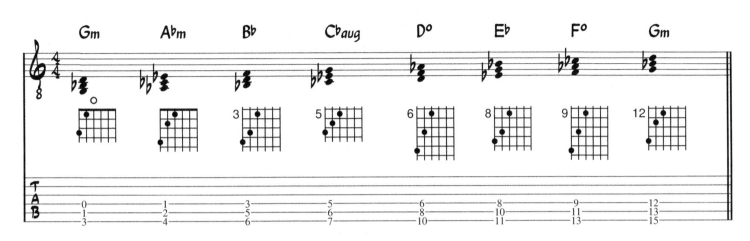

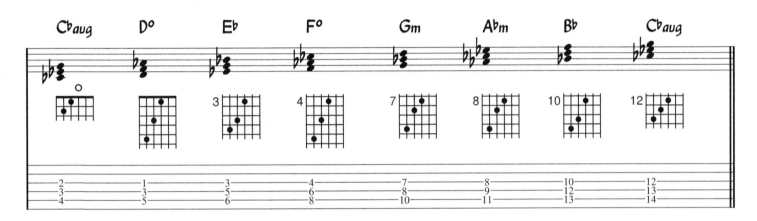

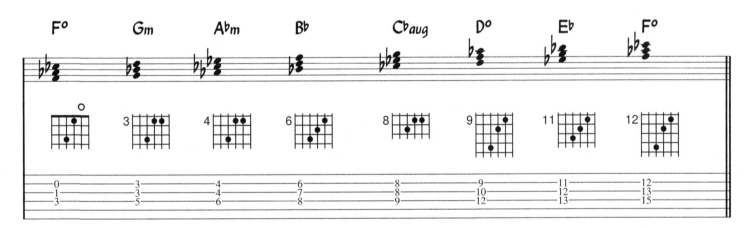

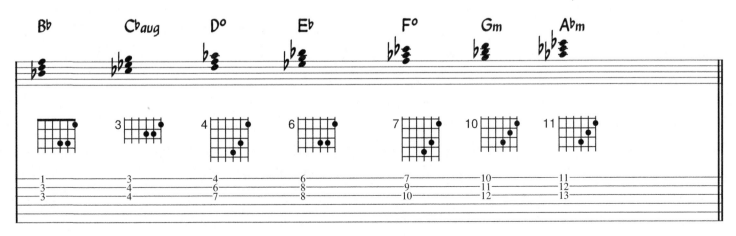

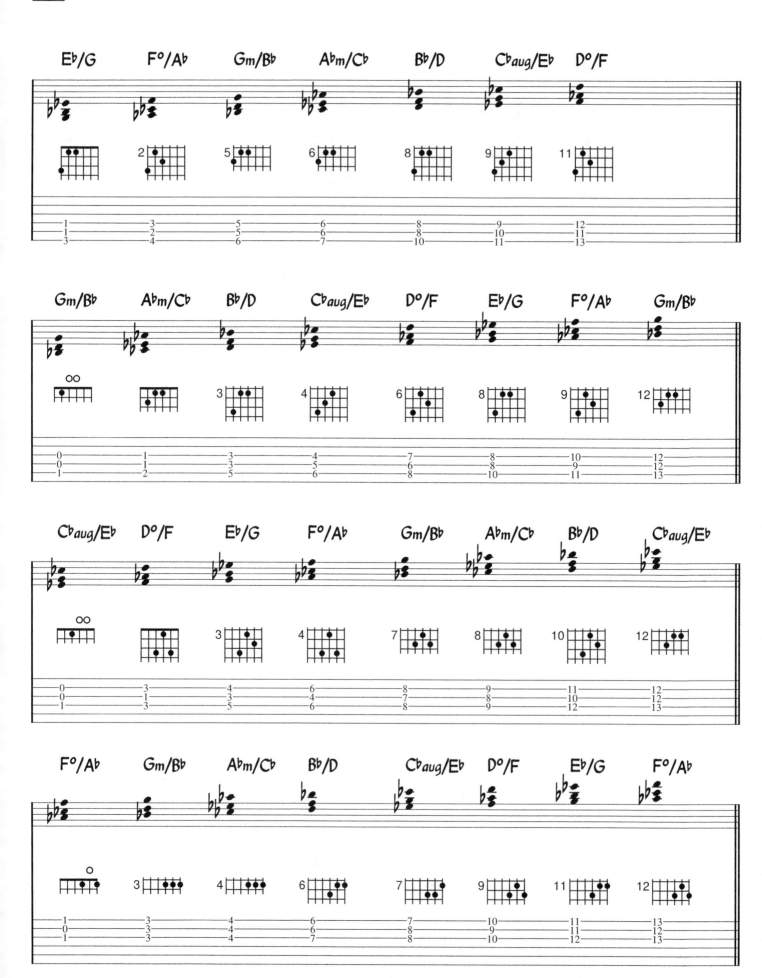

146

147

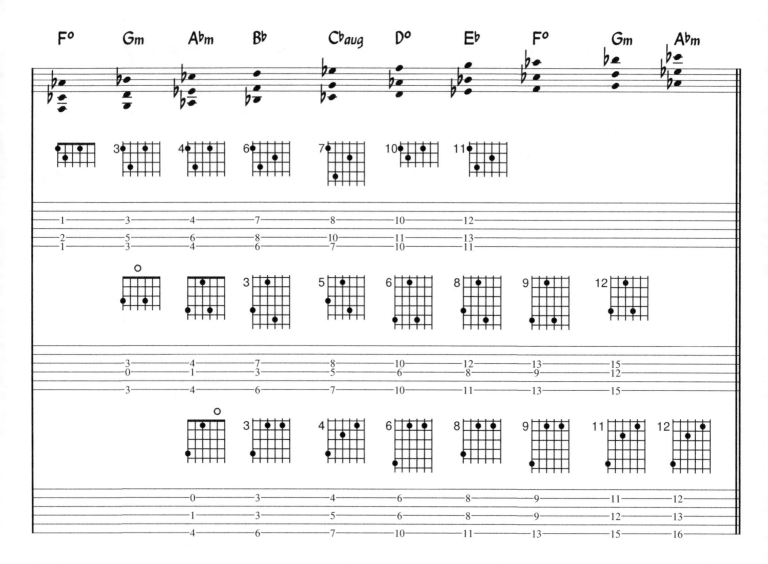

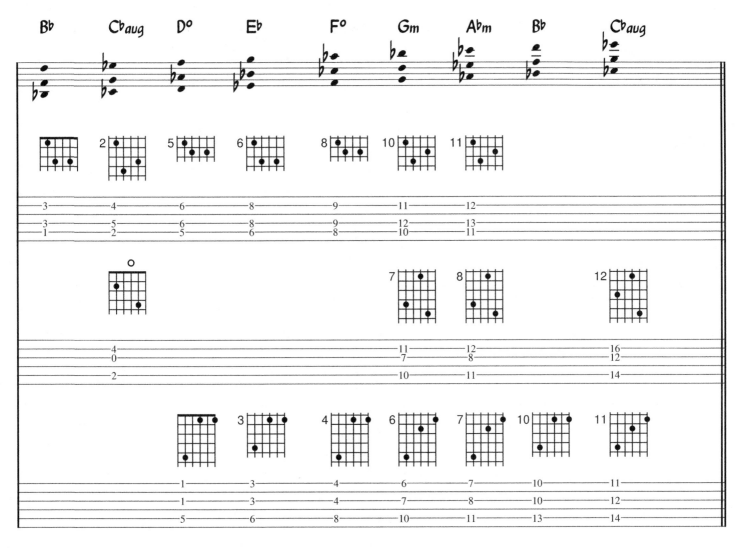

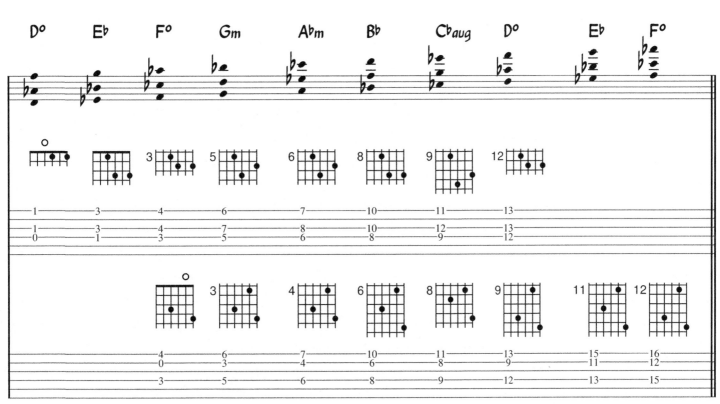

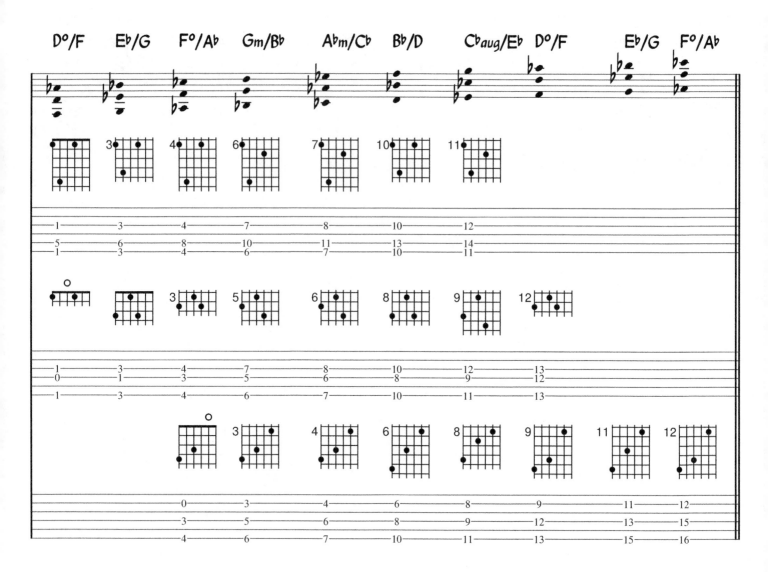

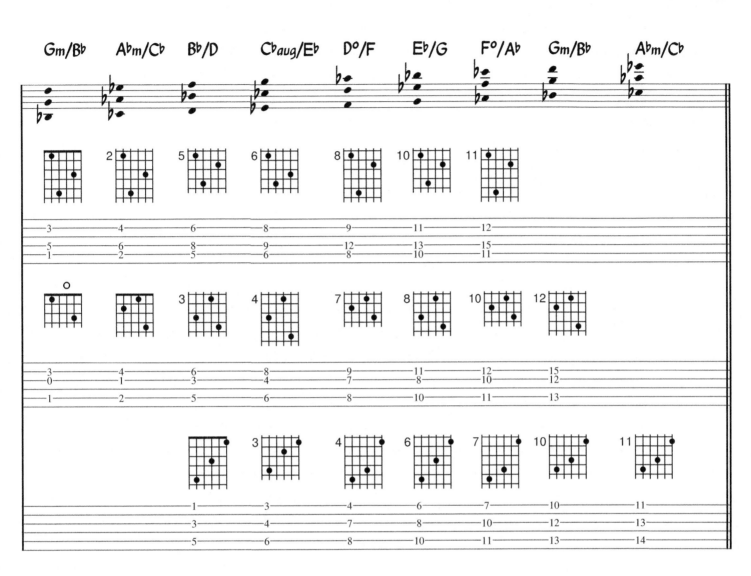

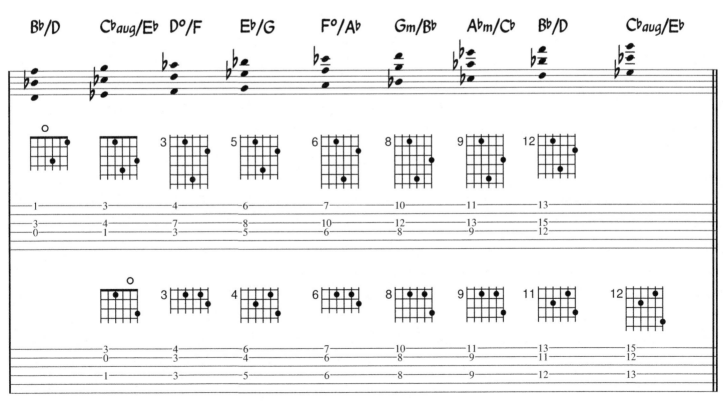

151

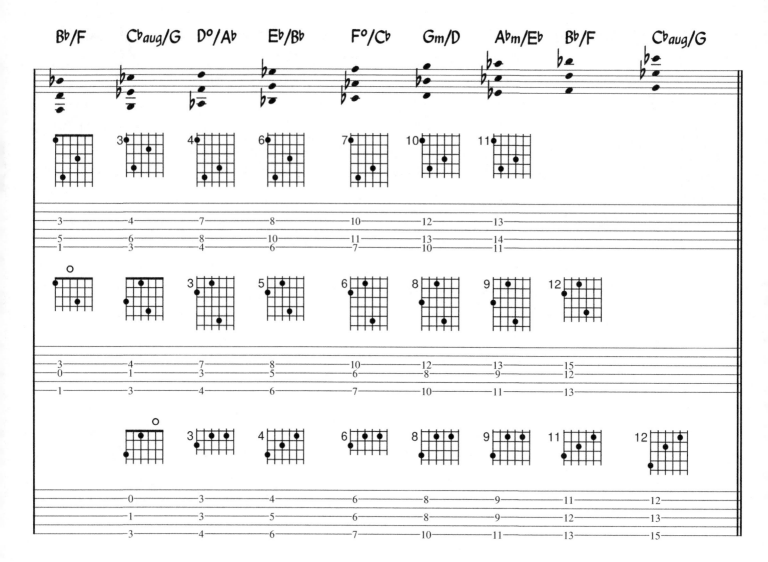

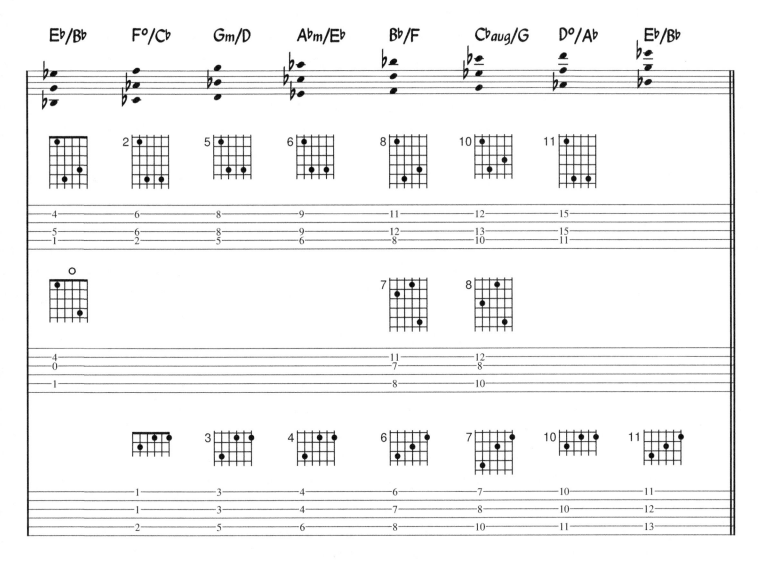

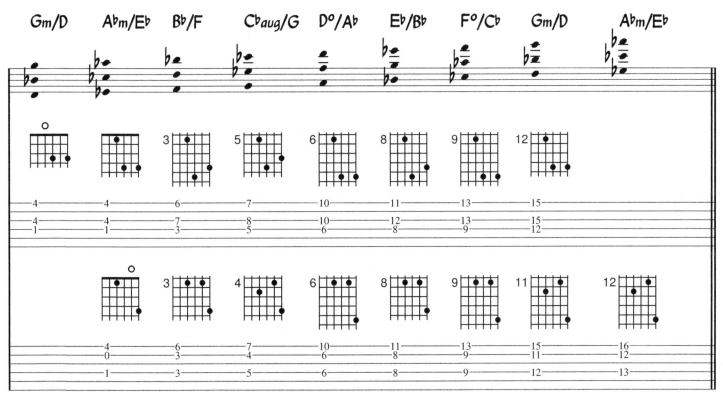

153

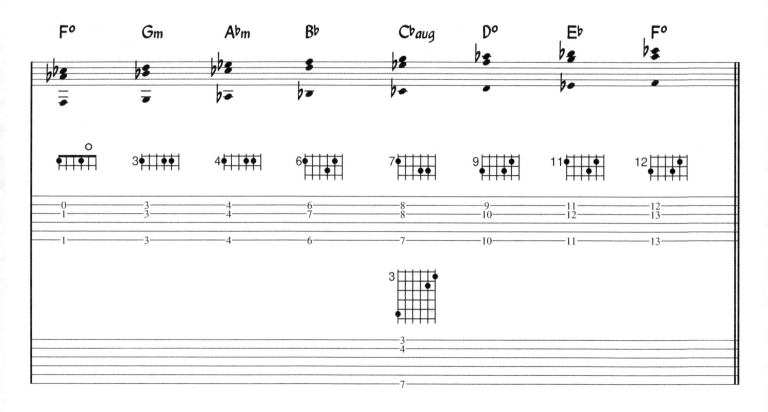

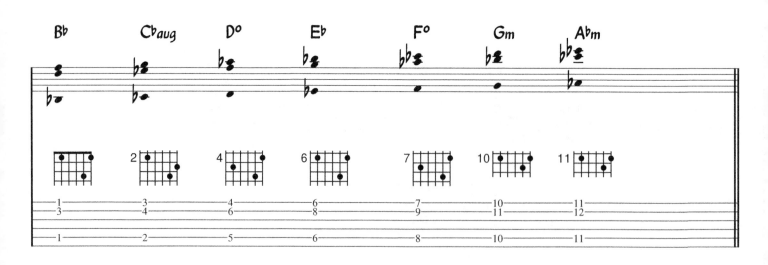

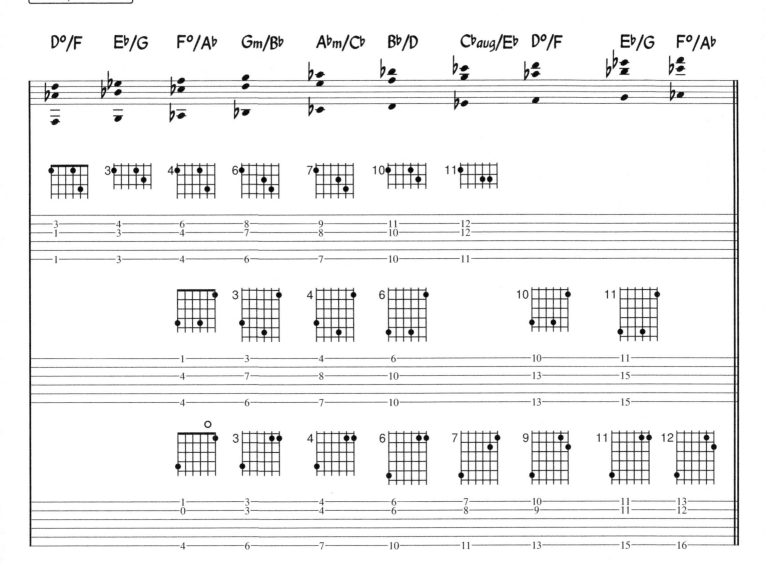

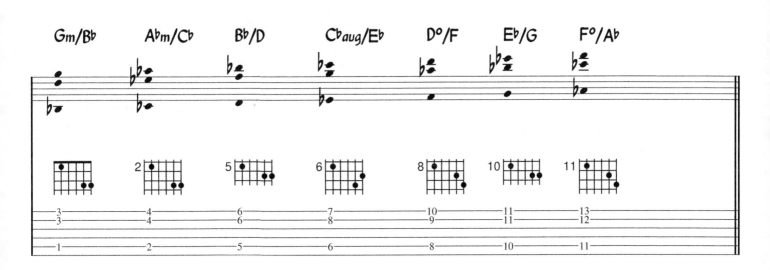

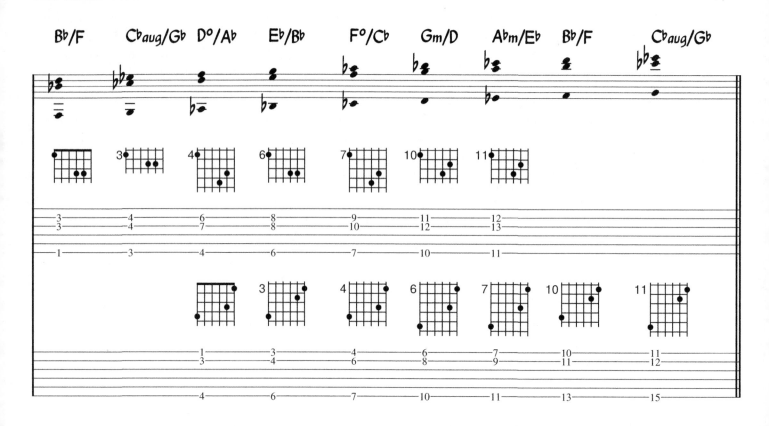

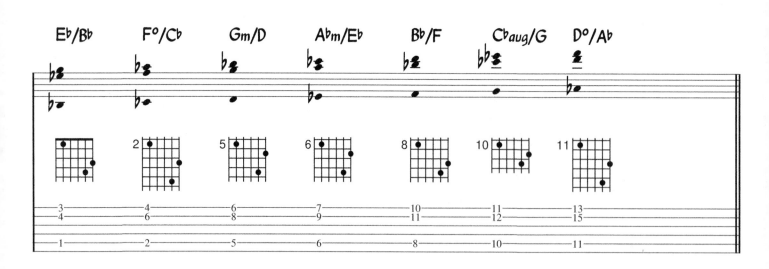

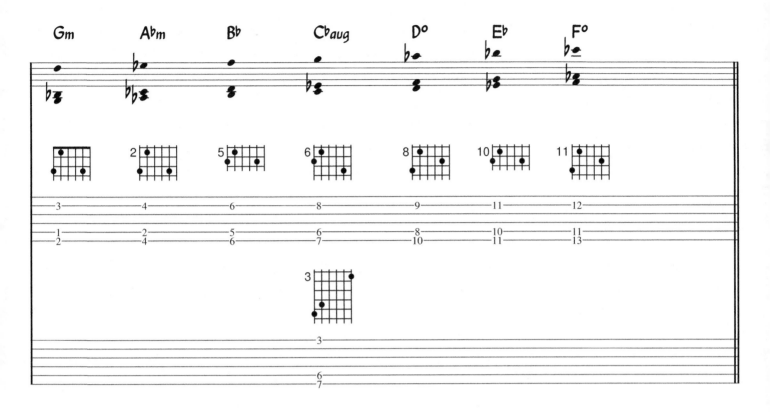

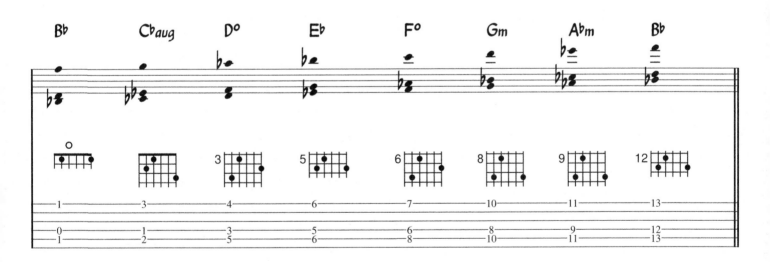

157

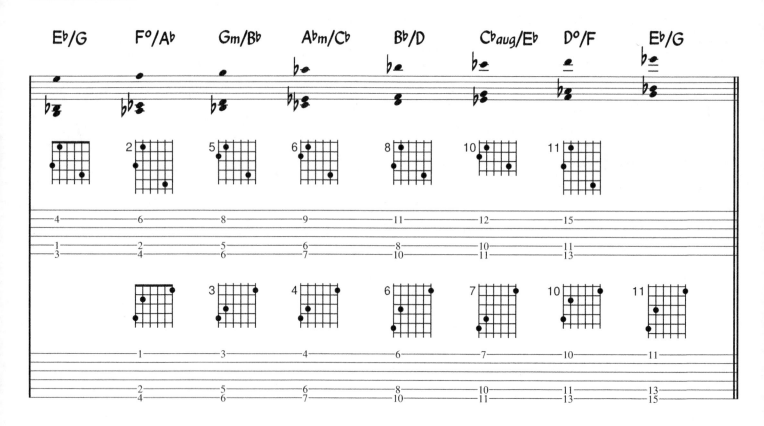

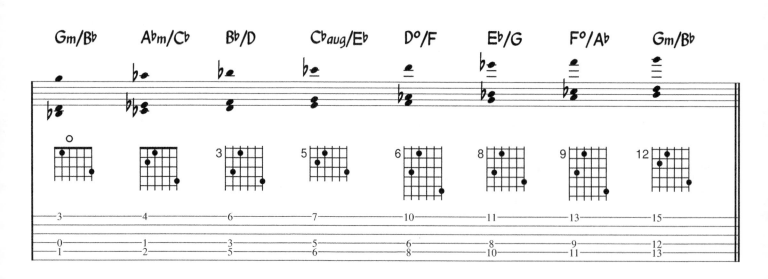

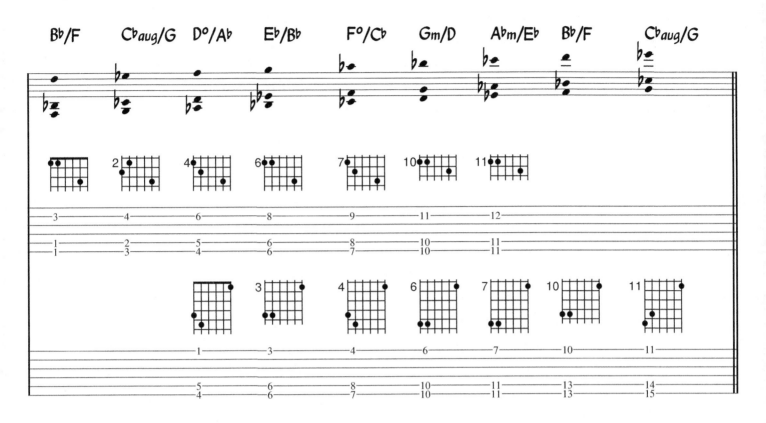

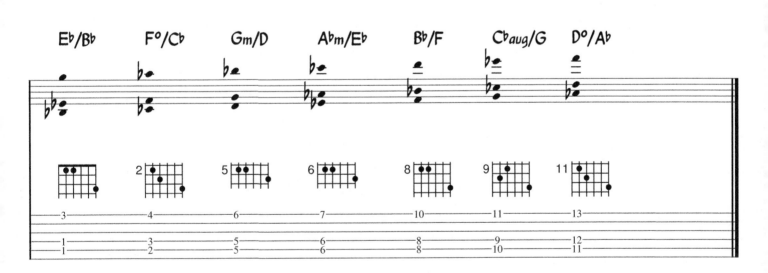

159

~ B♭ harmonic major ~

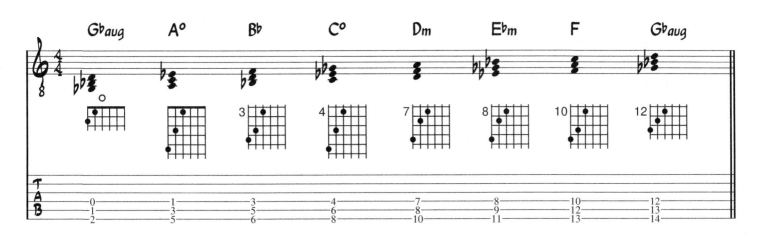

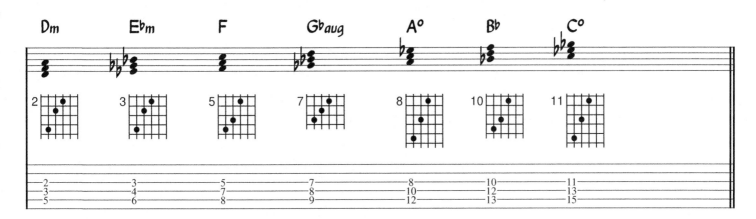

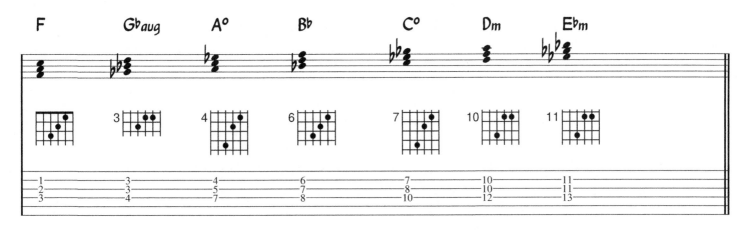

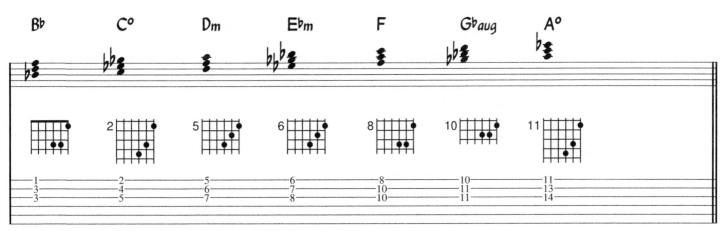

162

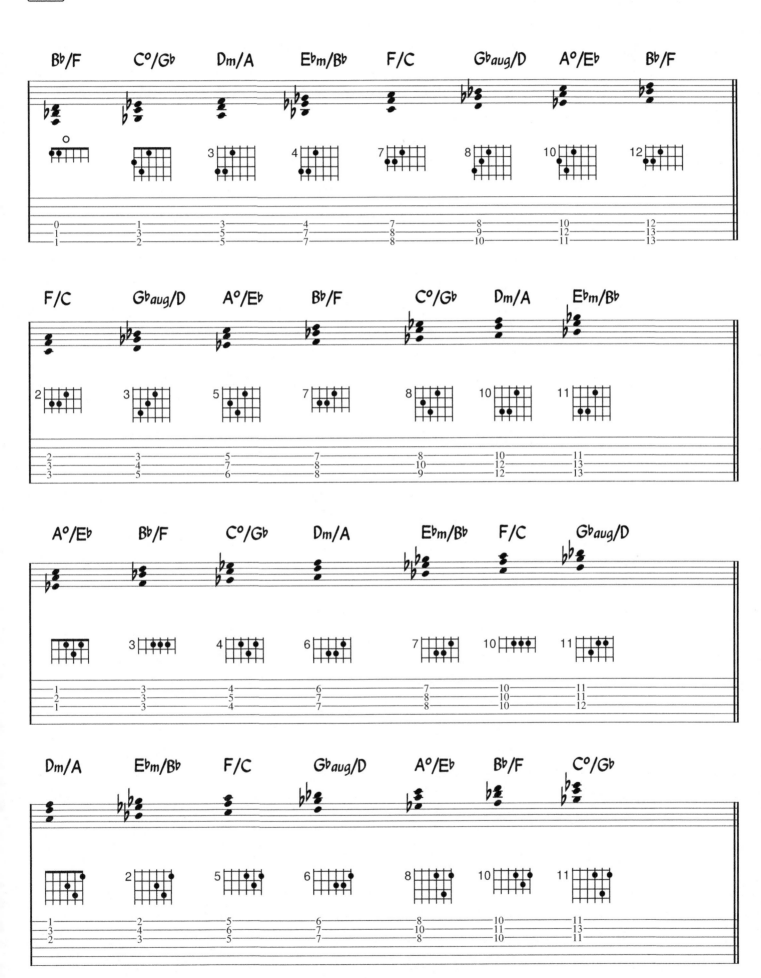

163

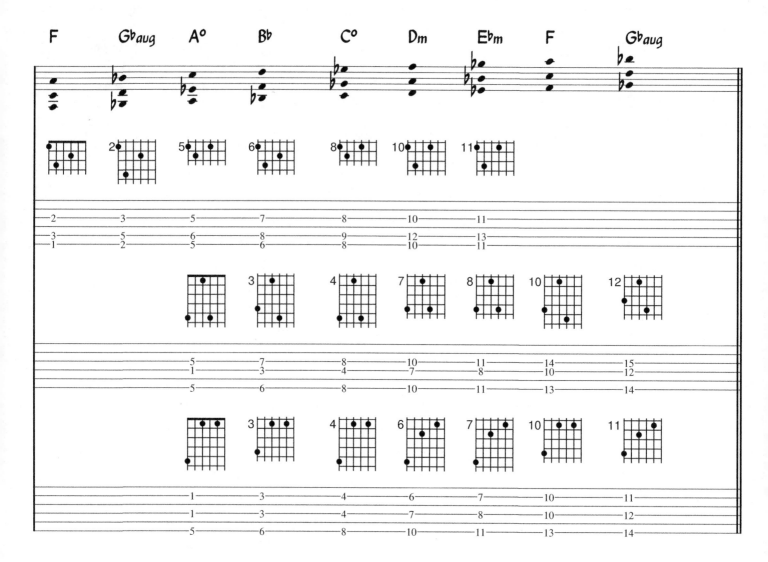

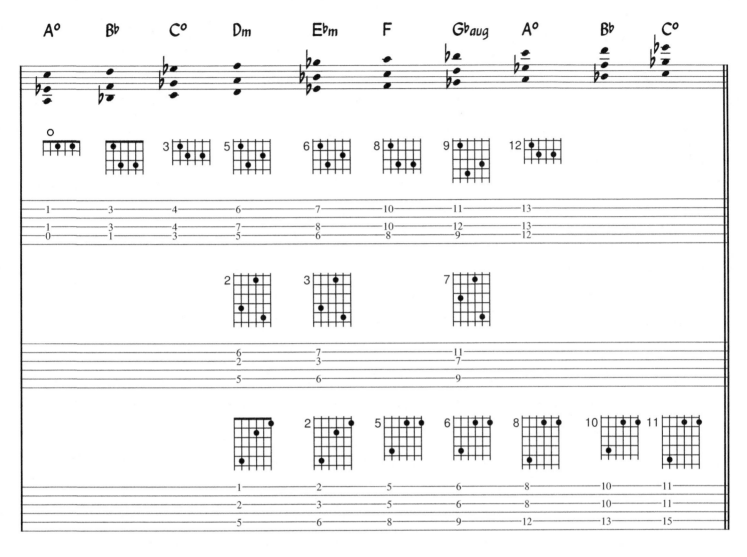

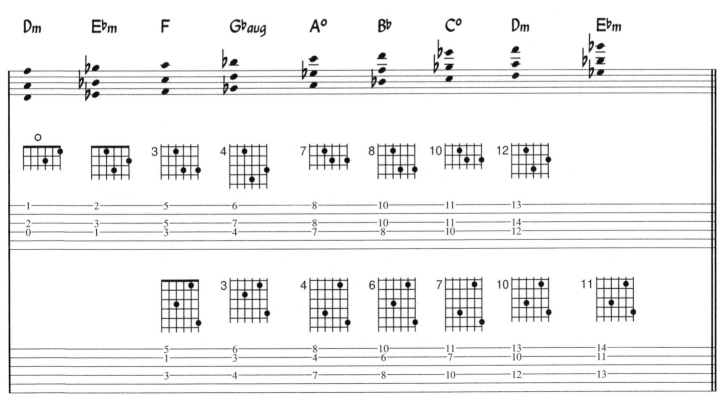

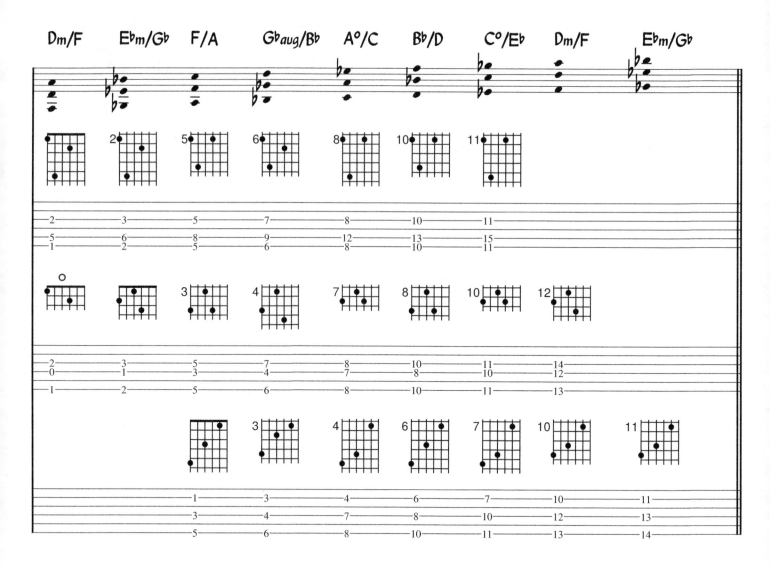

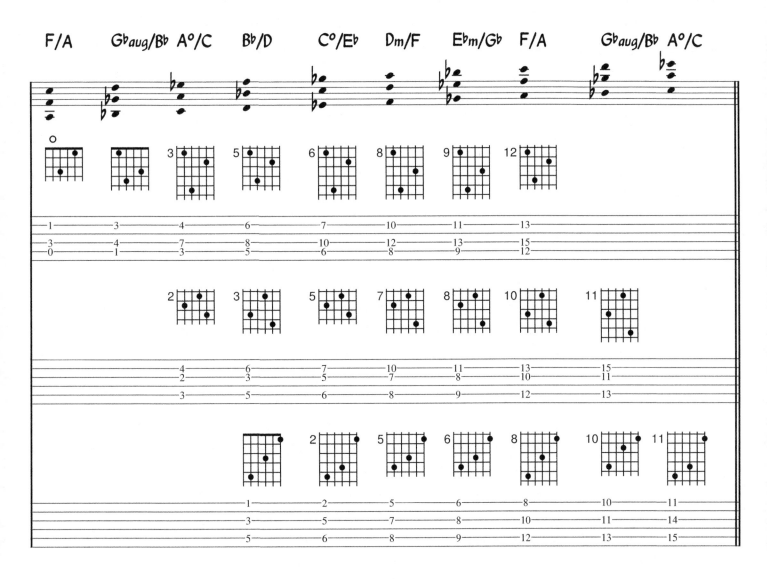

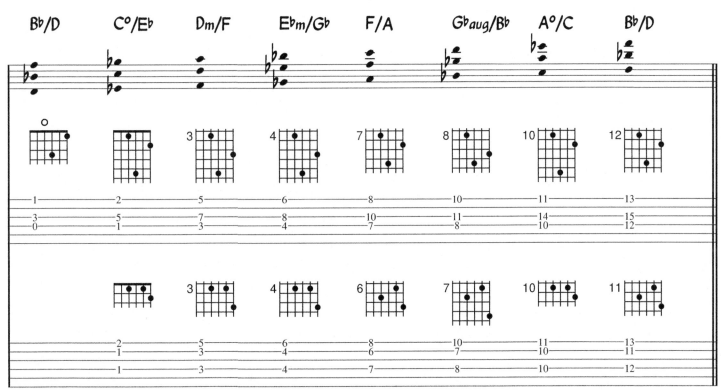

167

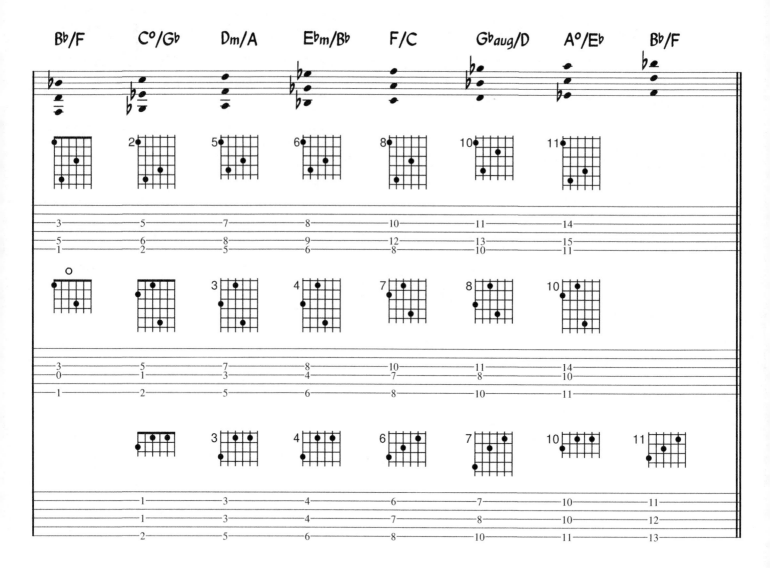

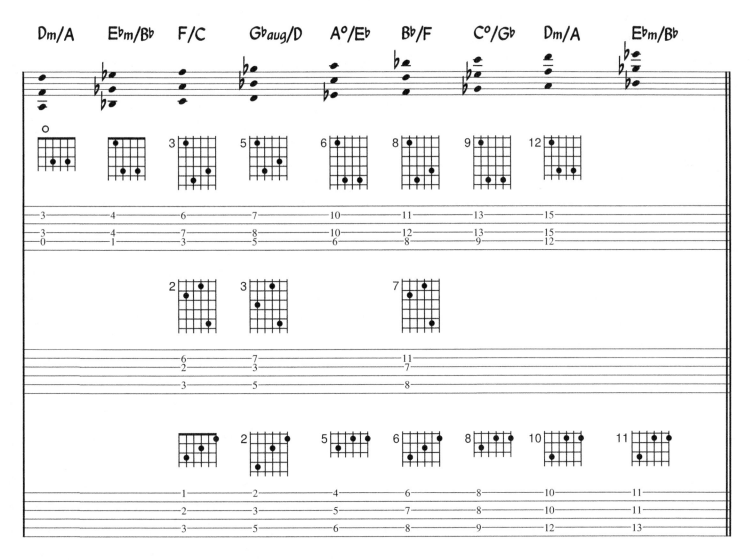

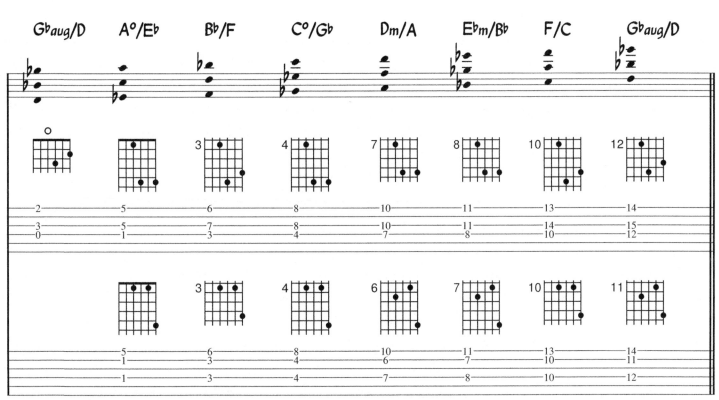

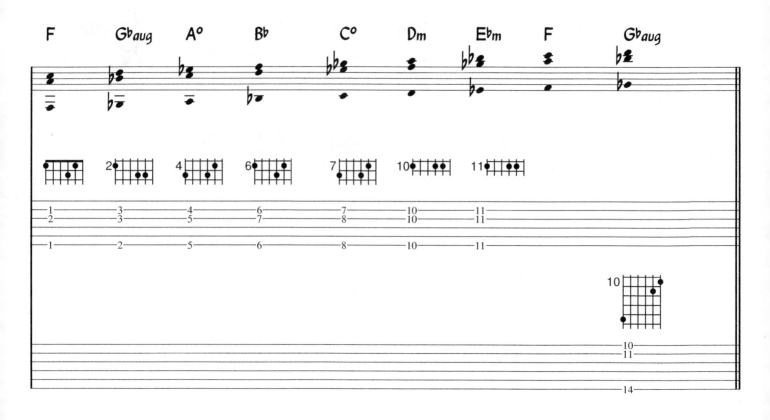

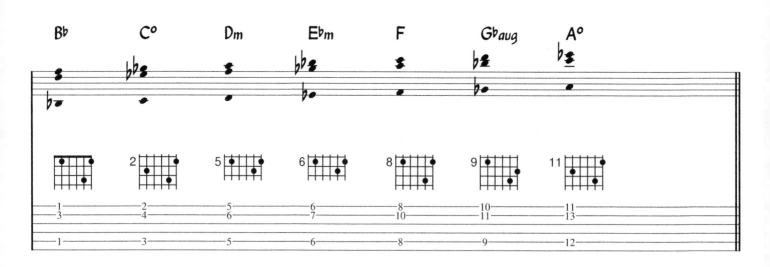

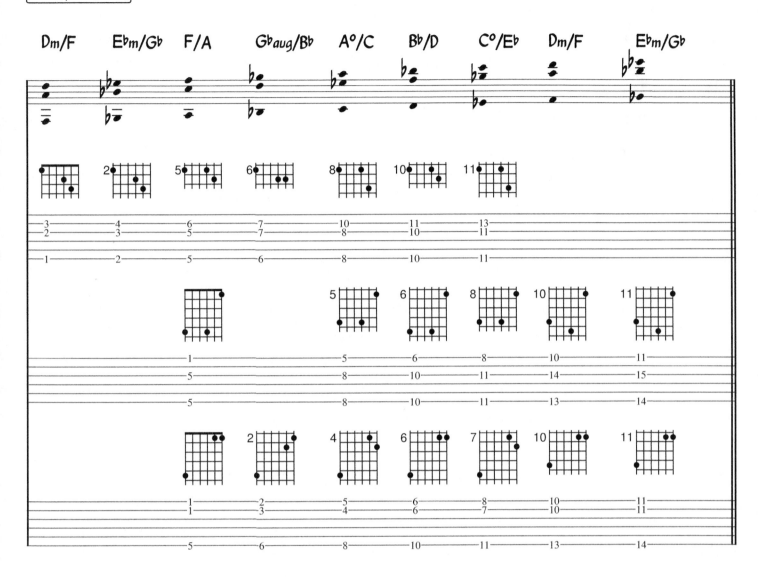

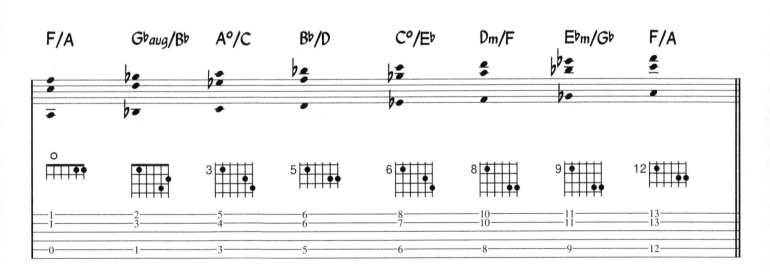

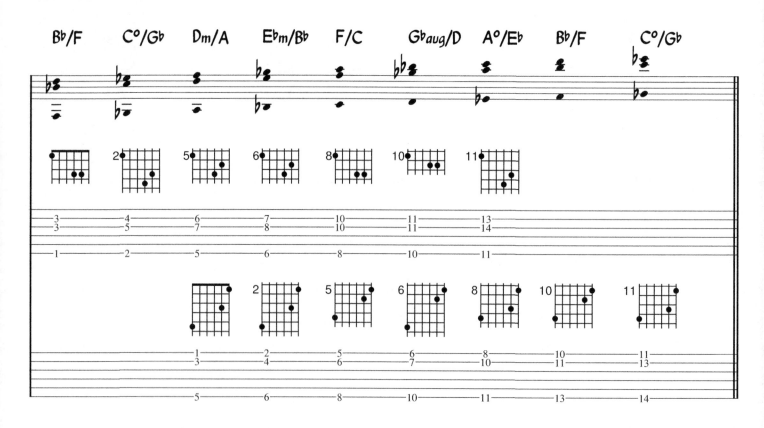

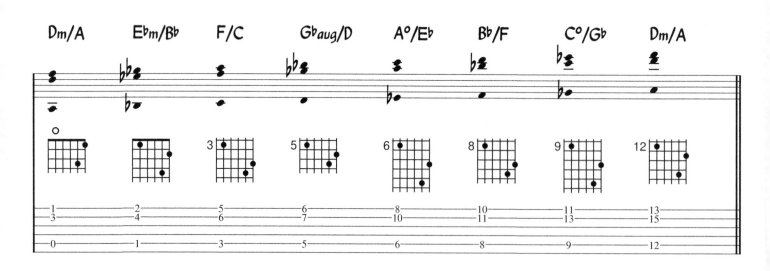

172

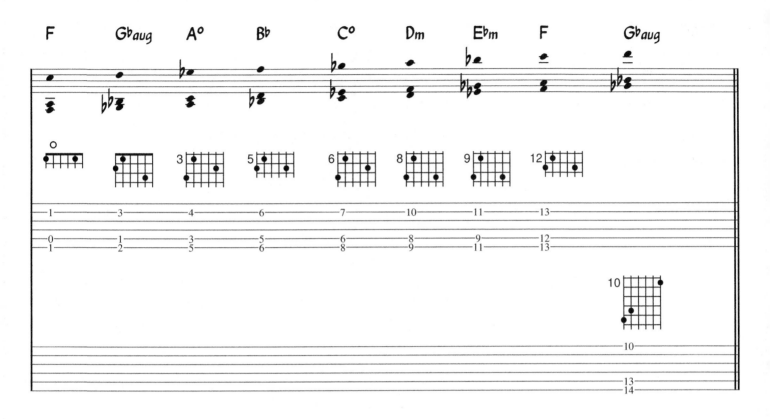

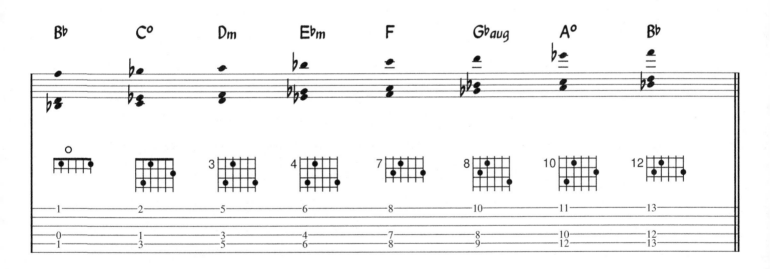

173

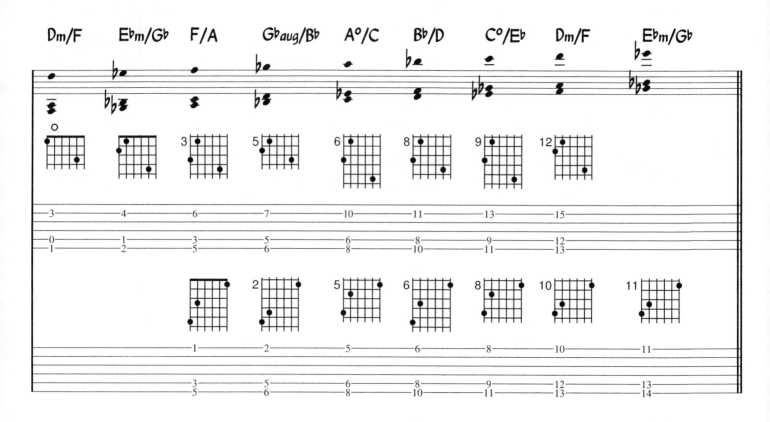

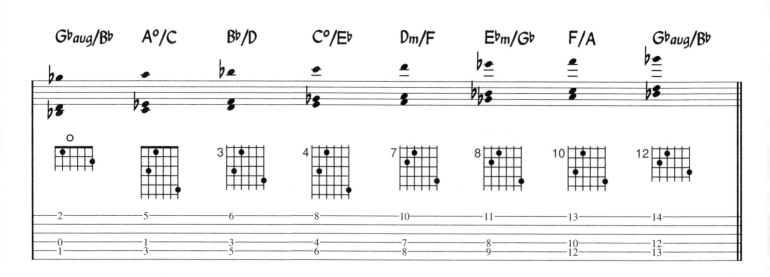

174

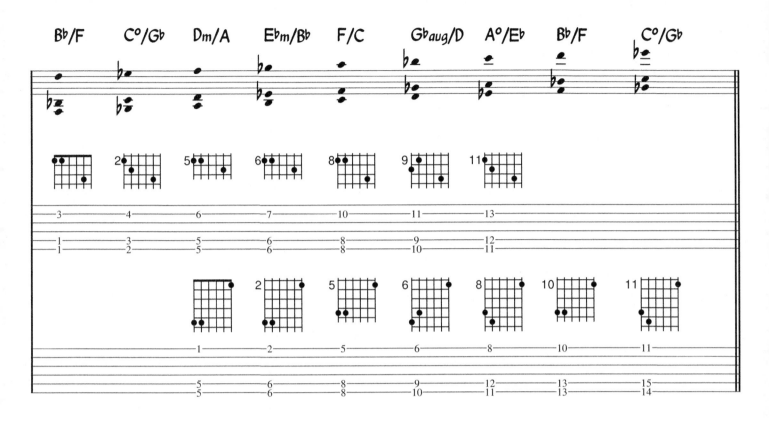

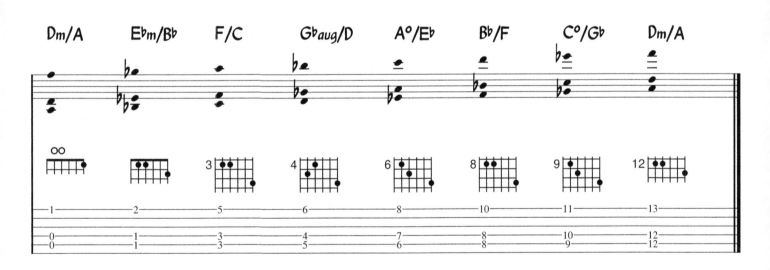

175

~ F harmonic major ~

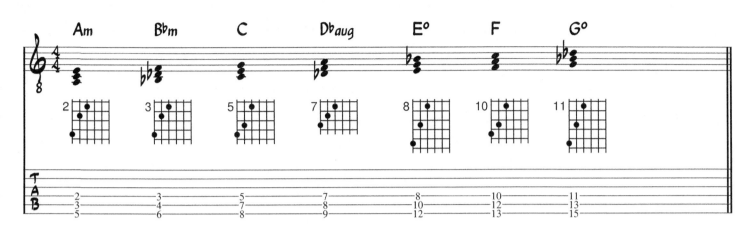

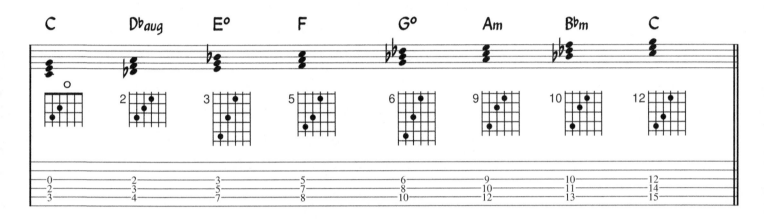

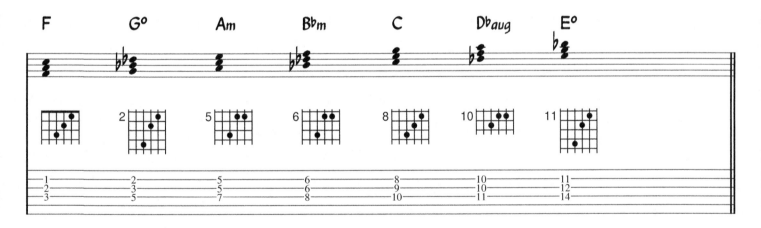

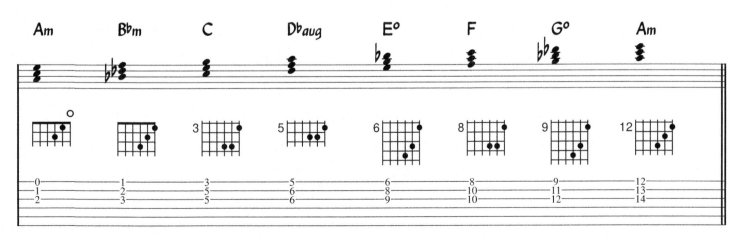

178

179

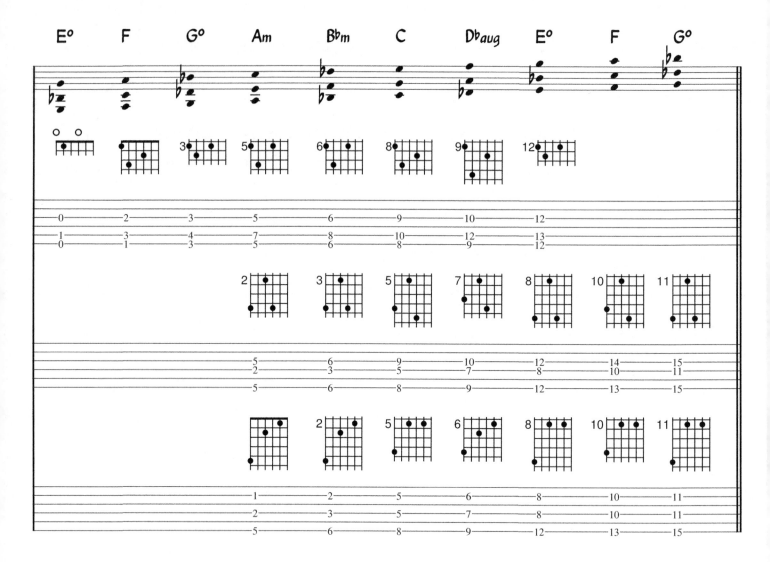

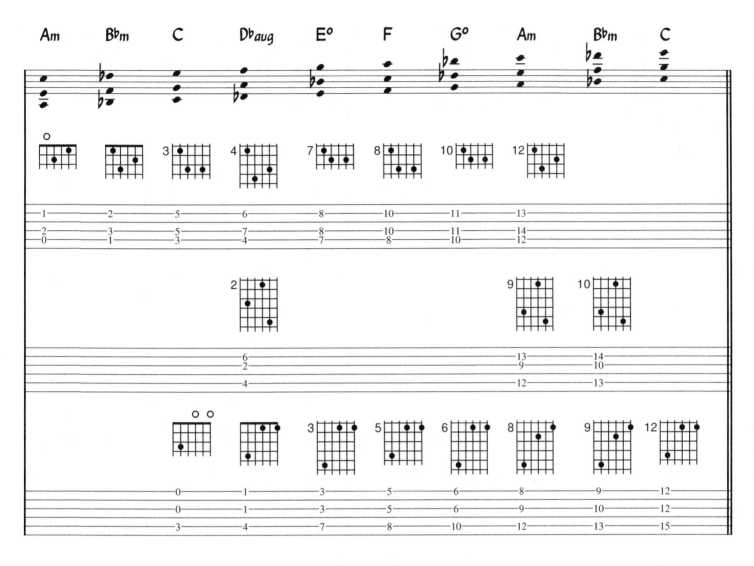

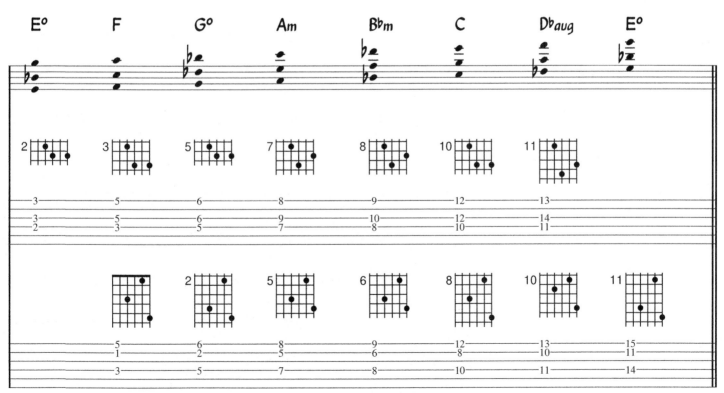

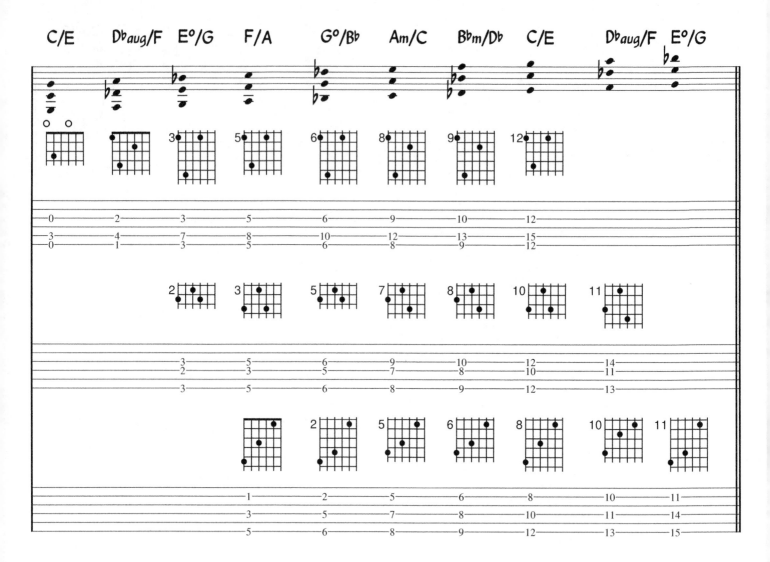

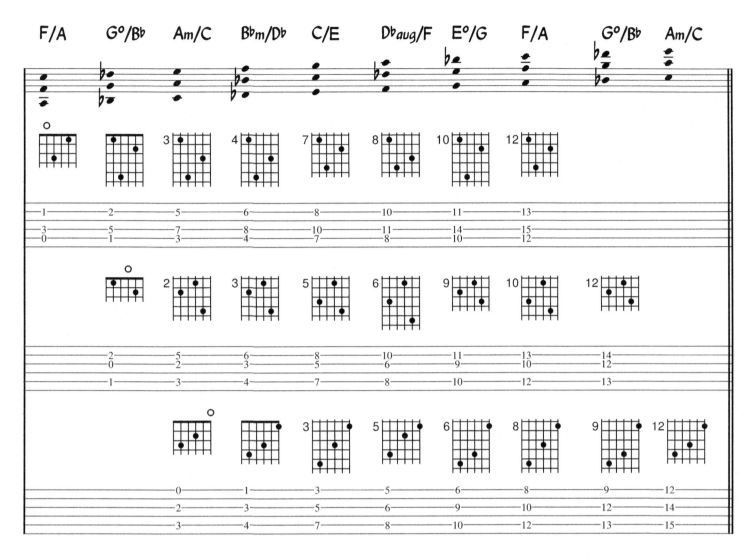

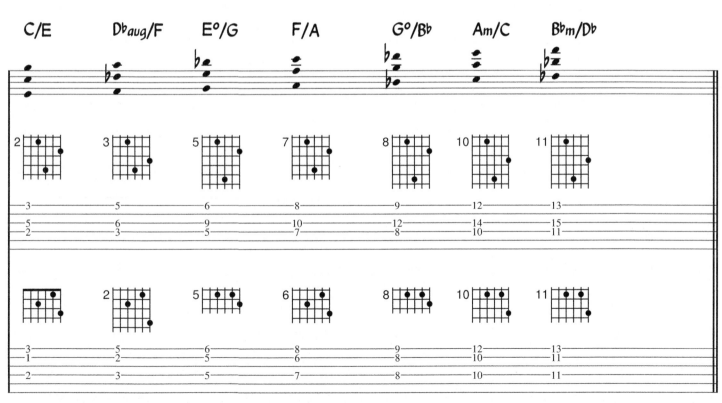

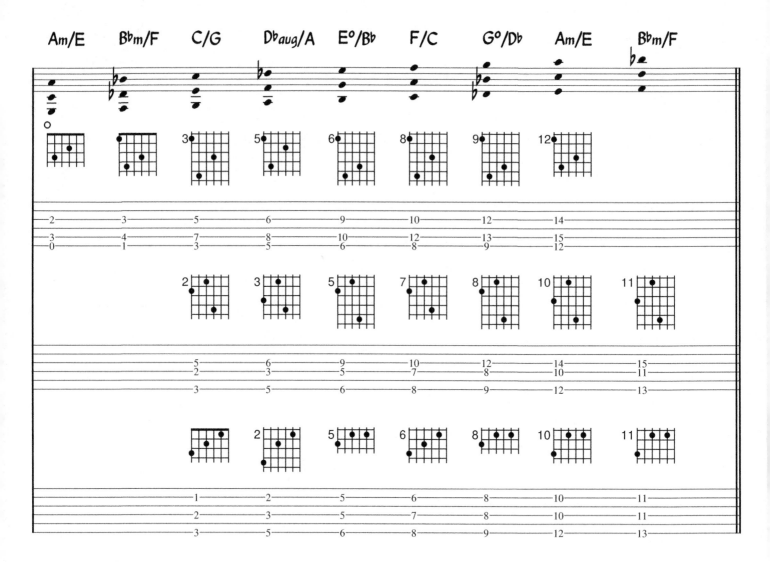

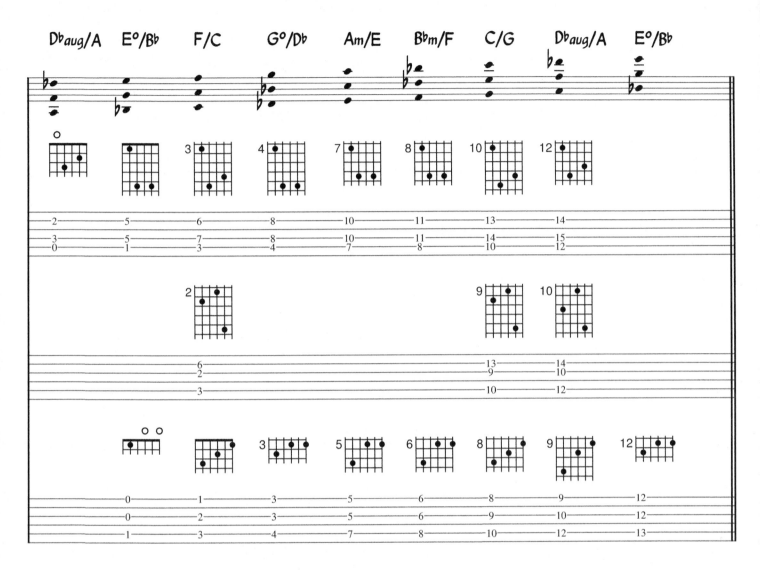

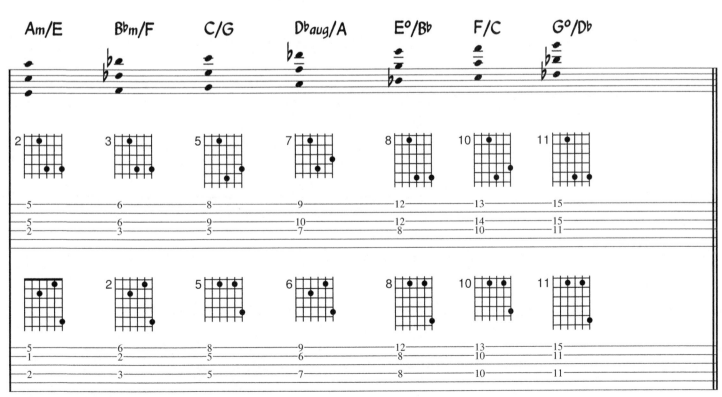

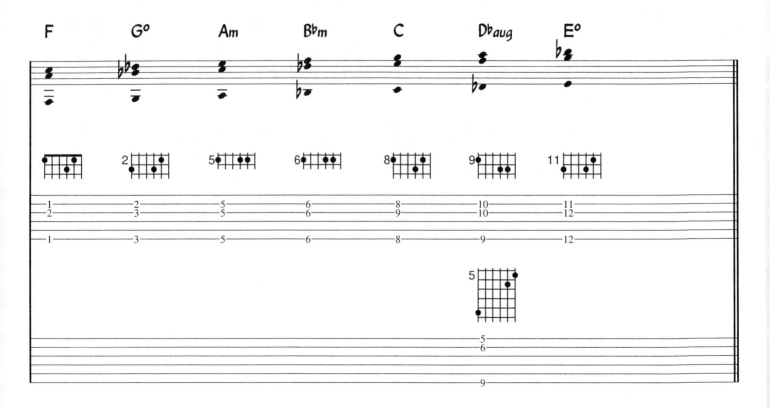

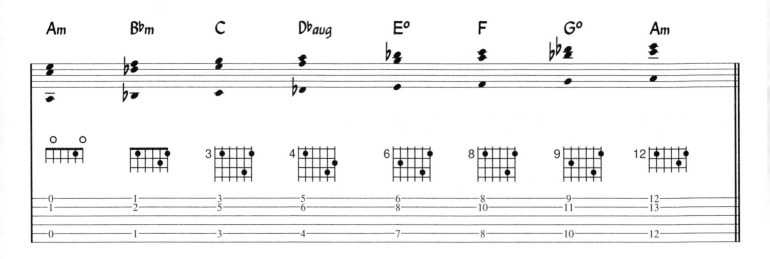

186

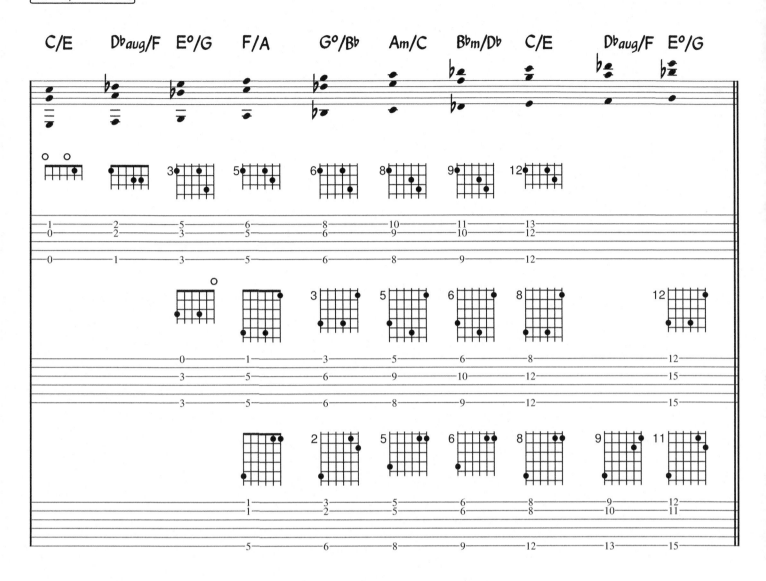

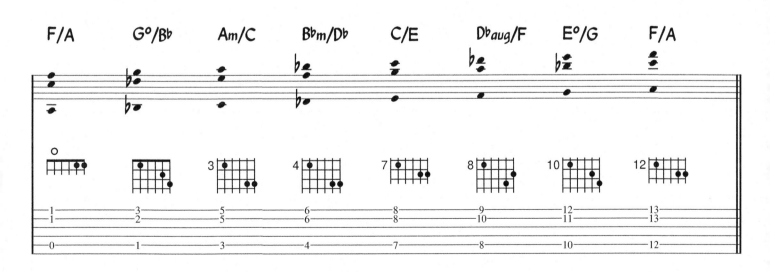

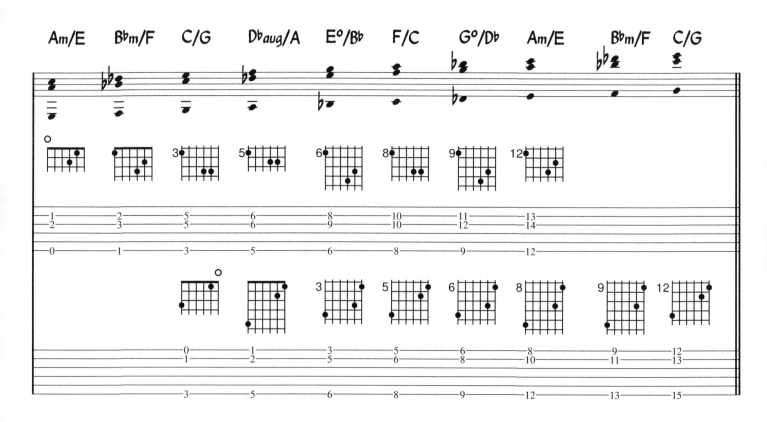

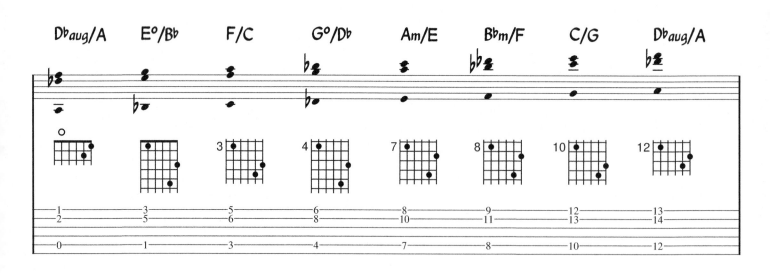

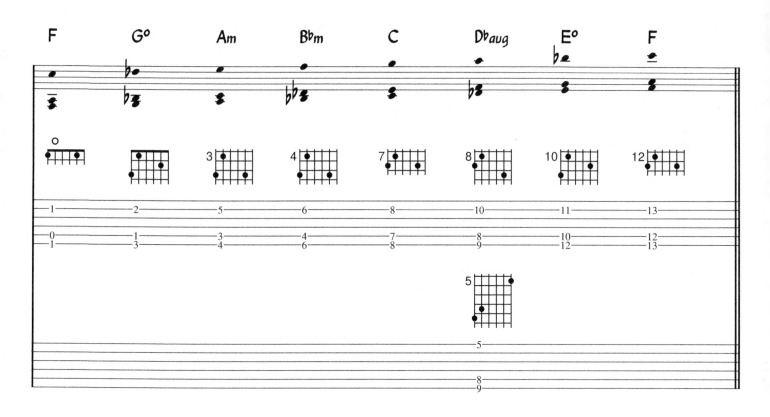

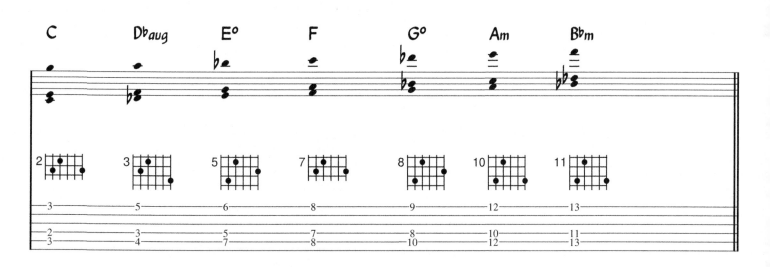

189

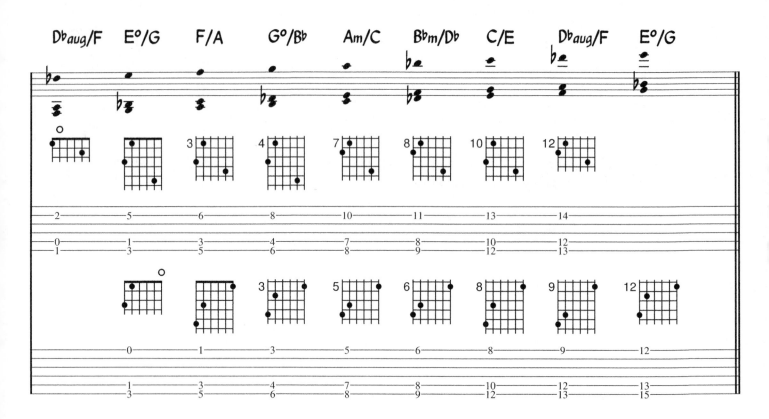

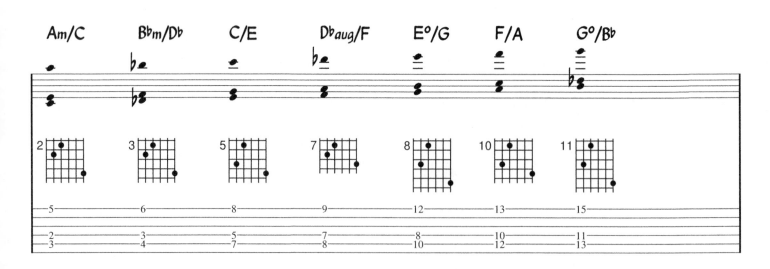

190

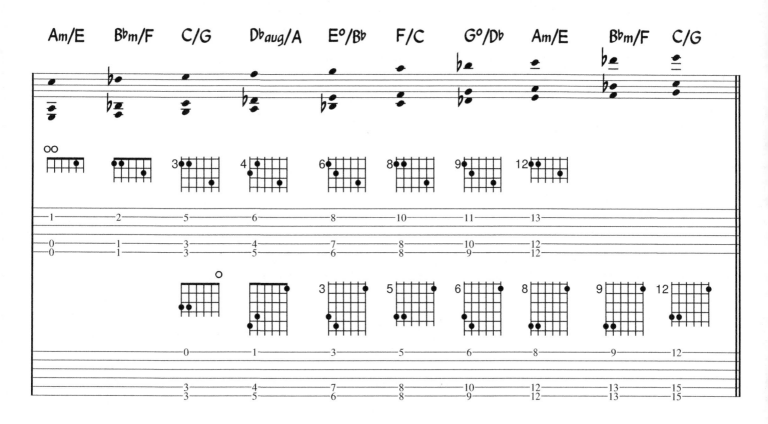

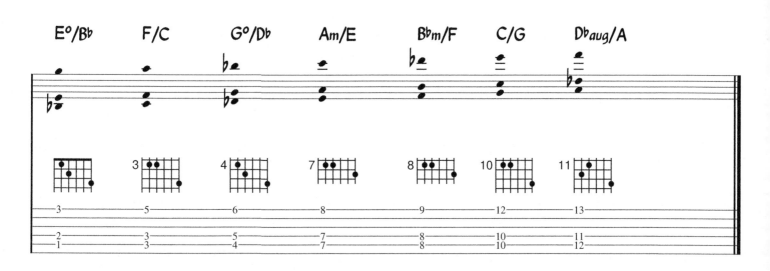

Printed in Great Britain
by Amazon

38813341R00110